Praise for SELF-ISH

"*Self-ish* is such a vitally important book for all of us—but especially women. At a time when social stressors have never been higher, and it's easy to find yourself slip-sliding on rocky terrain, this book could be a lifesaver. Dr. Sunita Osborn's real-life examples, straight talk, and helpful exercises show you how to find the kind of bedrock you need to be vulnerable but also engaged in today's world."

—**Kara Hoppe, MFT,** coauthor of *Baby Bomb*

"Dr. Osborn's book *Self-ish* is exactly what we need to start challenging the unhelpful and misguided narratives around taking care of ourselves. This is a must-read for every woman who struggles to prioritize herself and wants to find long-lasting strategies that she can put in place to live a meaningful and connected life."

—**Dr. Tracy Dalgleish,** clinical psychologist, relationship expert, author, and host of the *I'm Not Your Shrink* podcast

"Prioritizing yourself feels selfish and can be difficult for a lot of people, which is why this book is so important, especially in today's super-busy world. It's empathic, humorous, and filled with insightful guidance on how we can start caring for ourselves—without feeling guilty. Sunita explains concepts like self-love, self-esteem, and self-respect using anecdotes, research, and exercises the reader can use to reflect on themselves as they read and continue on their personal growth journey!"

—**Israa Nasir,** mental health educator, psychotherapist, and founder of the digital mental wellness brand Well.Guide

SELF-ISH

When Bubble Baths, Wine,
and Positive Affirmations
Aren't Cutting It

SUNITA OSBORN, PsyD

Published by
PESI Publishing, Inc.
3839 White Ave
Eau Claire, WI 54703

Cover and Interior Design: Emily Dyer
Editing: Chelsea Thompson
Layout: Mayfly Design

ISBN: 9781683736219 (print)
ISBN: 9781683736226 (ePUB)
ISBN: 9781683736233 (ePDF)

Printed in the United States of America.

CONTENTS

INTRODUCTION

I type "self-love" into Twitter, and immediately the search bar proclaims, "800 tweets in the last hour." Keep in mind, this was at 11:00 a.m. on a Tuesday—that's a lot of people thinking about self-love on a midweek morning. As a psychologist, I'm instantly happy about this.

Good for you, my virtual friends, I think, *out there thinking about what self-love means to you and finding ways to share it on Twitter. Let's see what you've come up with.*

As I start going through the stream of tweets under #selflove, a few stand out:

- "Crystals for self-love."
- "Your self-love gotta be bigger than your desire to be loved."
- "Self-love is revolutionary."
- "Self-love necklace."
- "Self-love over any type of love."

A few immediate impressions filter through my mind. First, I'm struck by how people are really feeling the "Your self-love gotta be bigger" quote. (We'll be back later with some thoughts on this.) Second, what is a self-love necklace?

Don't get me wrong; I love a good crystal as much as the next person, but I'm more than a little disturbed to notice a number of products for sale with the "self-love" tag. These tweets contribute to my overall concern and confusion as I continue to scroll.

You may be wondering why in the hell a psychologist is consulting Twitter about self-love. Rest assured—social media is not my primary source for defining self-love. What I'm trying to explore is how people understand their relationship with self, a fundamental concept that I always invite into the therapeutic space. You see, I've found that exploring and developing the relationship with self is one of the most helpful drivers of personal change. Clients asking questions (such as, "Why do I keep finding myself in relationships that ultimately fail?" or "Why am I constantly so hard on myself?" or "Why do I feel so empty when I have everything I thought I ever wanted?"), examining how they understand and express self-worth, self-trust, self-care, and other dimensions of the self-relationship, that is how we find answers, insights and, ultimately, a pathway for meaning.

Through these conversations, I have been fortunate to watch individuals reunite with parts of themselves that have been there all along but have been neglected or overshadowed by pressures and demands. I have witnessed their grief in realizing the numerous ways they were neglected or unloved growing up and how, thanks to that modeling and conditioning, they began to neglect and "unlove" themselves in seemingly innocuous but deeply impactful ways. I've also been witness to the joy and relief that comes from learning how we can create a relationship of unconditional love for all parts of ourselves (not just the pretty ones), a consistent sense of trust in ourselves to do the hard things (now and in the future), and a continual experience of care that goes beyond bubble baths and shopping trips to making difficult choices to prioritize our well-being.

Defining the Self-Relationship

The self-relationship is a ubiquitous topic in psychotherapy and, much like the other relationships in our lives, contains many complex layers. It refers to the way we view and treat ourselves, from responding to our body's signals to acknowledging ourselves when we experience adversity or triumph. Given the years of history we have with ourselves (in which we developed opinions, feelings, safety, trust, love, or care for ourselves through countless influential experiences), the clearest parallel to the self-relationship is the long-term relationships in your life.

Whether they be romantic or platonic, these kinds of relationships take continuous effort, reevaluation, conflict management, trust building, and showing up. The self-relationship also requires repair when you cause hurt or harm, as we all do from time to time; even here, the same principles from other relationships apply—you acknowledge how much this relationship matters to you, how you plan to do things differently, and you put those beautiful promises into action.

Despite this being the most central relationship in our lives, I've heard a lot of confusion from clients about the self-relationship, ranging from a lack of awareness that these relational concepts even exist (self-trust is usually a "Oh damn, that's a thing?" moment) to a realization that they don't even know what these concepts mean outside of the oversimplified version represented on social media. I've become increasingly concerned that our desire to share core psychological principles as like-worthy posts has compounded our collective confusion regarding the self-relationship.

Thus back to the search.

Hoping to alleviate the concerns raised by Twitter, I type "self-love" into the Instagram search bar and am confronted with 76.4 million hits. *All right, Instagram, I see you.* But my confusion only deepens as I'm assaulted with colorful posts, reels, and memes proclaiming:

- "Treat him like a king and nothing less."
- "Be positive. Don't be hard on yourself."
- "Gaslighting signs" with a list of behaviors and language to look out for.
- "Today is a new day. So sprinkle a dash of self-love with a hint of smartass and don't forget, a whole lot of badass."

While I thoroughly enjoy the last sassy quote, I find myself thinking, *How in the world do these ambiguous posts help people understand what self-love* actually *is?*

Now you may think that we shouldn't be learning about self-love from social media platforms anyway; we should learn it from our parents, our role models, or maybe even our therapists. While I agree in theory, my experience as a psychologist gives me doubts. I've heard many clients describe parents who were incredibly supportive and loving toward their children but seemed to lack this same attunement to their own needs. When I ask clients how they saw their parents show self-love, practice self-care, or nurture their self-worth, I'm often greeted with blank stares. I may also hear, "My family had no boundaries. Putting the needs of others above our own was praised, while focusing on yourself was considered *selfish.*"

Ah, the big bad word we all try our hardest to avoid. The word selfish has such a taboo attached to it—odd, considering that selfishness is essentially just acknowledging you have a self to focus on. (More on this later.)

Social media is a wonderful avenue for both information seeking and interpersonal connection. During the pandemic, social media allowed us to maintain and develop connection during a time we needed it badly. We've also seen the power of social media for supporting history-making movements as various platforms became hubs for deeply important and vulnerable storytelling.

Of course, every good thing has its flip side. As much as social media can be the ultimate source for seeking, sharing, and distributing information, it can also be the ultimate source of misinformation and inaccuracy. This is particularly relevant when we think of key psychological concepts that carry so much potential impact for individuals' lives. The more these vital concepts are distilled into succinct "shareable" posts, the more we risk losing their original meaning or, worse yet, misunderstanding them altogether. Think of it as the world's most dangerous game of telephone, with each new post (based not on the true definition, but on a previous post) becoming more and more distant from the original meaning.

Whether these core concepts have become so widely misunderstood through their social media saturation or through internalized beliefs from intergenerational patterns, we've drifted further and further away from a true understanding and felt experience of these concepts. Consequently, we are missing out on what embodying these concepts could do for our overall quality of life and sense of purpose and meaning.

The Why, the What, and the Who

This book invites, reveals, and leads to greater understanding of the true and unfiltered domains of the self-relationship by utilizing psychological theory, academic research, clinical cases, and of course, a witty sense of humor. Together, we'll explore all the dimensions of the self-relationship in all its vital nuance, identifying origins, meanings, and actionable, sustainable ways you can embody each of these dimensions throughout your life.

Let me say it again: this work is meant to be done *throughout your life.*

Many resources out there offer pithy tips on how to improve your self-esteem, self-control, and self-discipline. Some of those tips are even offered in this book, though they may not be as short. However, best believe what they lack in brevity, they make up for in depth, because the kind of long-term impact I know we all want takes committed practice as we continue to grow.

Because the relationship with the self is a long-term one, the insights and exercises in this book are not meant to be one-and-done, but rather read, considered, executed . . . and then executed over and over again, until you've developed "muscle memory" that allows you to leave this book on the shelf. (Until you need a reminder, that is.)

I hope you will pick up this book when you are moving through a huge life transition, whether ending a relationship, starting a new job, finding the you that has been neglected for years, or looking for a deeper awareness of self. It's also the book I hope you pick up when you feel like your life has everything you could have ever wanted—the great job, the great house, the great family—but you are still not feeling fulfilled.

Now get ready to meet you.

Self-Love

Merriam-Webster Dictionary: *An appreciation of one's own worth or virtue.*

Urban Diction ary: *Being selfish, thinking about and doing stuff for yourself more, and before, other people, and doing what you love for yourself. Self-Love is only good and acceptable when you've done everything you can for other people, that you have time to yourself, and you can do the things you love.*

APA Dictionary of Psychology: *1. Regard for and interest in one's own being or contentment. 2. Excessive self-regard, or a narcissistic attitude toward one's body, abilities, or personality.*

(Definitions may be paraphrased from sources noted.)

1

SELF-LOVE

Why We Start with Self-Love

There's a reason why my Twitter search started with self-love, and it's not only because the term auto-populated as soon as I typed the word "self." Possessing love for yourself is the essential foundation for the hard, transformational, soul-deep work we are beginning together. Similar to the foundation of a house, the presence and stability of self-love is required to uphold the weight and stress the self -relationship (that is, the house) puts on it. Also like the foundation of a house, self-love cannot be expected to stay in pristine condition for decades without proper maintenance.

Unfortunately, we often neglect the maintenance of our self-love even worse than our home's foundation. Assuming it's a given, we pay little attention to developing, nurturing, or even checking in on it. However, Google search data suggests we still think about this concept often. Global internet search trends suggest that interest in the topic of self-love has many spikes throughout the year, with a noticeable peak around February (specifically around Valentine's Day). We can assume this has to do with 1) a holiday focused on love, forcing people to examine their relational choices, and 2) media messaging that heavily pushes the narrative of how important it is to love yourself over everything (. . . And here are some crystals to help you do just that!).

While I am not expecting you to constantly descend into the crawl space of your psyche to assess the foundation of your self-love (okay, I promise the house analogy ends here), it is essential that you continue to maintain and reinforce your self-love so that it can evolve and grow with time. This is especially important as the complexity of developmental stages and life's challenges also evolve and grow with time. A solid foundation of self-love is what allows us to meet these challenges at our best.

What Self-Love Is and What Self-Love Isn't

As previously discussed, there are many fun, engaging, and quite relatable social media posts out there on self-love. However, as with many of the concepts we will discuss in this book, just as many posts share distortions and misinformation on this topic. Even the American Psychological Association, the go-to resource for mental health professionals, seems to be divided in their understanding of this concept. Their first definition calls self-love "a regard for and interest in one's own being or contentment," while their second meaning reads, "Excessive self-regard, or a narcissistic attitude toward one's body, abilities, or personality." Talk about confusing!

One of the challenges in defining self-love is making the definition succinct. Self-love is a broad term that encompasses a way of being, thinking, and acting toward yourself. It includes internal acceptance of unpalatable thoughts and emotions as well as actions that show warmth and unconditional regard for yourself, such as allowing yourself to cry without reproach after a hard-ass day.

Another challenge in defining self-love is how easily it can be confused with self-indulgence, e.g., your friend's Instagram post that reads, "I bought this handbag because I deserve it #self-love." Now, I'm all about some indulgence (my recent purchase of cowboy boots reflects this); however, self-love does not mean giving yourself whatever you want when you want it.

A parent does not show her child love through acquiescing to every single desire. Instead, she shows her love by responding to the child's needs and showing unconditional care, even when her child throws down her sippy cup for the eighteenth time or screams bloody murder when mommy won't let her play with the Tylenol bottle. This parent may feel annoyed as hell when these things happen and respond with some type of consequence or behavioral redirection; but love and care remain at the core of her interactions with her child. She understands that this child isn't fucking with her just for fun, but rather is learning how to handle "big" emotions and experimenting with different methods to get what she wants.

And guess what? Even when that child becomes an adult, she still will likely throw tantrums, make a mess, and probably have a host of equally embarrassing fuckups. At that point, her own self-love will guide her to respond with grace and compassion toward herself.

Bottom line, self-love does not mean giving yourself a hall pass for bad behavior or catering to every pleasure-seeking desire you have; instead, it means recognizing that in your humanity, you will do things you admire and feel deeply proud of *and* have thoughts and commit actions that feel terrible to recall. Thus self-love means consistently valuing who you are as a person. It means honoring your needs, acknowledging that you are figuring things out as you go, and recognizing that you have the capacity to continue growing each and every moment into the badass you are.

Love Yourself Before Others Can Love You: The Greatest Lie Ever Told

Now that we have a clear idea of what self-love is and isn't, let's get into one of the greatest lies ever told. That comment from Twitter sums it up—the one that was so well-liked that it came up multiple times on my #self-love search: "Your self-love gotta be bigger than your desire to be loved."

While self-love is certainly important—so important that I have a whole chapter dedicated to it—the dangerous part of this quote is its suggestion that we should quantify our self-love in comparison to the love we desire from others. In my clinical work, I have heard so many clients deprive themselves of the love and comfort of others based on the conviction that they need to be completely in love with themselves before they can be loved by another. I find this such a tragedy. We are not born with the capacity to love ourselves—it is through being loved, cared for, and made to feel safe that we develop the autonomy and ability to form a healthy self-relationship, which includes self-love. In other words, our self-love comes about by allowing ourselves to be loved, seen, and valued by others.

An additional note here: this doesn't mean all is lost if you haven't had people in your life who consistently gave you the love and care you deserve. It just means this is the conditioning to pay attention to as you work to make changes in your life.

In case my soapboxing isn't enough to convince you, let's consult attachment theory.

Developed by John Bowlby and Mary Ainsworth (1979), attachment theory is the science of relationships that explores how we develop, maintain, and experience connection with others and ourselves. Attachment theory posits that we are born with an innate desire to connect with others and have secure attachment with them, meaning we feel safest when we are around our primary caregivers. We may feel distress when they leave, feel happy upon their return, and seek them out for comfort and play. A fundamental aspect of developing a secure attachment is experiencing *mostly* consistent love, care, and acceptance from our primary caregivers. Receiving this type of care from others is how we develop and maintain our self-love.

The "mostly" is in italics because none of us will be able to respond to each other or ourselves with love, care, and attunement 100 percent of the time. Research assures us that we only need to respond this way 30 percent of the time to maintain a secure attachment (Tronick, Als, & Brazelton, 1977). It's the quality, y'all, not the quantity.

As an example, let me introduce Cynthia, a well-spoken real estate agent I worked with for several years. She was all about the self-help world—she had read all the books, knew all the lingo, and was very much about ensuring that her "cup was filled" (a refrain she used frequently during therapy). Cynthia believed that part of filling her cup was not allowing herself to date, even though she did desire to be in a relationship, because she needed to "truly love" herself before she could be in a healthy relationship. I gently called "B.S." on this line of thinking and helped her understand why being in relationships with others (whether romantic or platonic) would actually support the self-love she was trying so hard to cultivate.

As humans, we are wired to be in relationships. We are herd creatures and need others around us in order to survive and thrive. While Cynthia was doing amazing work on her own, exploring different parts of herself and providing them with love and compassion, she needed to see that the love and care of others could be instrumental in showing all these parts of her that they had value. I pointed to our therapeutic relationship as an example of how another person's loving, caring presence had encouraged Cynthia's journey of developing self-love. We discussed how the important self-work she was doing would not end when she entered a relationship—rather, the relationship would help it evolve.

Cynthia did eventually begin dating and had many beautiful moments of connection, along with (of course) many challenging and painful moments of disconnection. The outcome of her romantic journey, while important, paled in comparison to the wealth of reinforcement, experience, and self-knowledge she received—enough to fill her cup to the brim.

Why Self-Love Can Be Challenging for Women

> *I should be able to handle the responsibilities of having a job and taking care of my family.*
>
> *I shouldn't show I'm upset; they're going to think I'm weak or too emotional.*
>
> *If I can't have a baby, does that make me less of a woman?*
>
> *If I don't want a baby, does that make me less of a woman?*
>
> *I don't just have to perform as well as my male colleagues—I have to be better.*

Any of these thoughts sound familiar? As women, we are faced with a host of "shoulds" from day one. We are told we should be sweet (i.e., we need to take care of everyone else first), we should be pleasant (the acceptable emotions we can display are happiness, serenity, and calm, and maybe some fear too, because how endearing is that?), and we should be able to do it all (we must perform at top capacity at work while also ensuring that our home life is cared for with the same level of ferocity that we show in that boardroom presentation). It doesn't help that the concept of womanhood is often synonymous with motherhood, which means being unable or unwilling to have a child is grounds for questioning one's identity as a woman.

Taken together, these expectations create a conditional standard of love that is unique to women. As a result, our love for ourselves often becomes based on meeting these requirements. It's almost as if, based on all the messaging (implicit or explicit) we were and are exposed to, we decided on a pristine job description for being a woman.

In my mind, it would go a little something like this:

Job Description: Top Duties and Requirements

We are looking for an enthusiastic, agreeable, always pleasant woman to join our team!

To be a successful woman, you should be able to assess the emotional needs of everyone around you and intuitively know how to respond, as per your training as a nurturer for every living thing around you. In addition, you should have a thriving career where you are beloved by all, and not allow the very real systemic biases in your workplace to impact your success or likability. You should also have a beautiful homelife with 1 to 2.5 children and a supportive partner, and you should ensure that even though you may have the same workload as your partner, you are doing at least 1.5 times as much household-related work as they do. (If you don't have the same occupational workload as your partner, you must do 8.5 times as much household-related work as they do.)

To apply, please share your social media pages so we can assess how well you fit these requirements. We can't wait to meet you (or not)!

Take a moment to imagine what other qualities or responsibilities or duties you would add to this job description. Perhaps certain physical qualities should be included, or additional personality traits women must have in order to be valued. The expectations we put on ourselves create a conditional sort of self-love—that is, we believe we are allowed self-love *only* when these conditions are met.

As discussed previously, self-love is the foundation needed in order to take risks, make mistakes, and be generally human. Conditional self-love, on the other hand, causes uncertainty, anxiety, and shame, and can manifest into behaviors such as perfectionism as we strive to reach and exceed each impossible expectation set for us.

The conditions we create for self-love are not easy to abandon. They were cemented into our minds from years of conditioning, either explicit or implicit, from our families, our communities, and certainly social media. These conditions are reinforced well into our adulthood across settings and contexts, making them nearly impossible to set aside. But while we cannot always rid ourselves of these ideas completely, we can choose to notice and learn from them. That feeling that you could truly love yourself if it weren't for those few little parts you wish you could get rid of? That's where self-love work really gets interesting.

What's the Hardest Part of You to Love?

You have no bad parts. Yep, I said it—take it in. Every single part of you was developed to fulfill a certain need. The creative part of you that helps you see and solve problems in a way that no one else can is the same part that helps you turn a mundane evening into an UNO tournament with side bets, standing ovations, and passionate team allegiances. But while it's easy to love the parts of you that help you be successful and bring praise from others, self-love also means valuing and nurturing the parts of you that are hardest to find compassion for.

We all have a particular voice within us that is mean, critical, even downright hateful toward ourselves at times. In general, we call this the "inner critic," though some people even give theirs a name. ("Karen" is a popular choice these days.) This inner critic is not only mean, but also indiscriminate with its timing. It shows up when you are stressed about that presentation at work, reminding you of all the times you fucked up in the past, taunting you with the memory of your coworker's killer presentation that had everyone talking for days after. It also shows up after you ace your presentation to caution you against getting full of yourself, then replays the "tape" on your performance so you can review and dissect every micromovement you made. So yeah, that inner critic gets around.

Interestingly, the inner critic isn't nearly as polite or pleasant as it insists *you* should be. When the inner critic decides it is needed, it bulldozes past all the other parts of you to take the wheel and primary control of your immediate internal reactions and external behaviors.

Some signs that may alert you when your inner critic is making its way into the driver's seat include:

Physical signs:

- Tightness in your chest
- Rapid breathing
- Sweaty palms, sweaty underarms, sweaty everything
- Digestive issues
- Headache
- Shaky voice
- Trembling body movements

Mental signs:

- Difficulty concentrating
- Racing thoughts
- Feeling "caught up" in your head or as if you have blinders on
- Debating with yourself (inner critic part likely debating with another part of you)
- Negative perception of your abilities, capacities, and person

Reading all this, you may be thinking, *Yes, exactly! This part of me is the absolute worst. Boo, inner critic!* However, remember how we discussed that self-love isn't just loving the "easy" parts of yourself? It's loving every single part of you—yes, even the inner critic.

To begin changing your relationship with the parts of you that are hard to love, let's explore how they came to be.

Stop Shaming Your Inner Critic

Internal family systems therapy (Schwartz & Sweezy, 2019) posits that each of our parts, similar to members of a family, contain valuable and meaningful qualities that have the capacity to benefit the entire system if utilized well. For instance, we have "protector" parts that develop during childhood to guard us from the outside world and keep us safe within the group we belong to. These protector parts fall into the categories of managers or firefighters. We'll explore the firefighters in Chapter 4; but for now, let's get to know our managers.

We keep our emotions and wayward thoughts in check to prevent us from being hurt or rejected. Your manager makes sure that your behavior doesn't get too out of hand, that your words or tone don't offend anyone, and you are generally likable enough that others want to get close to you and take care of you. Over time, your manager gets so good at their job that they become fixated on the specific task of impression management—that is, making sure that everything you do is "perfectly" right and criticizing you if you step out of line. This isn't because your manager wants to make you miserable. Quite the contrary—your manager realizes that if you don't listen to their feedback, you are not going to get your needs met.

What compounds this cycle is that those around you may like it when your manager is in the driver's seat. Your parents appreciate your compliant behavior, your teachers praise you for getting every question right, and your boss says she wishes all her employees were as "perfect" as you are. The manager hears this and chimes in, "Ah, see? Look at all the praise and love we get when I look out for you."

Of course, there's a flip side to this. Let's say the playful part of you wants a turn in the driver's seat. Your manager thinks about it: *Hmm, things have been calm enough lately. People like us, our needs are met. Sure—get on in there, you!* (In my head, the manager sounds like a paternal cowboy.)

Your playful part decides to have some fun at work. Instead of focusing on the agenda during the team meeting, the playful part decides it would be fun to start a game of "Would you rather" with your coworkers. Everyone has a great time, and it seems to be a beneficial team-building exercise after how stressful things were during the last quarter. Later though, your boss pulls you aside and chides you for derailing the meeting. Sensing your needs are in danger, your manager immediately gets back in the driver's seat and berates your playful part for negatively impacting your boss's perception of you and potentially threatening your livelihood.

Over time, this cycle becomes familiar—you come to expect the manager to show up anytime you make a mistake. Even if you haven't done anything "wrong," you anticipate the manager waiting in the wings to point out something you could have done better.

Understandably, over time, you begin to loathe this part of you—you become a big fan of those Instagram memes that advise things like, "Tell your inner critic to shut the f*** up. It has nothing to say that you need to hear."

Still, no matter how many times you try to shame your manager/inner critic into silence, they always comes back with a judgment to make on what you are saying, wearing, or even thinking.

Love this part of you yet? That's okay. We've still got some work to do.

Your Misunderstood Manager

My first real job was working at a fashion retailer in the mall. I got to see my friends, and I got a 40 percent discount on everything in the store—a dream job for me. The only non-dreamy part of it was my store manager, Esmerelda, who had very exacting standards for how her employees behaved on the job. Not only did she watch us like a hawk, but she remembered every time we made the most minor mistake and seemed hell-bent on reminding us that each of these mistakes could put our jobs in jeopardy.

I assumed Esmerelda must have hated her own tedious role so much that she had to find pleasure in her own limited power over us. That, I reasoned, was why she commented each time I didn't upsell the store's credit cards, or didn't put the clothes from the dressing room back on the racks fast enough, or didn't say, "Welcome!" and "Hope you have a great day!" with enough enthusiasm. (Man, I sound like a terrible employee. No wonder Esmerelda was always on my case.)

As it turned out, my assumption wasn't too far off. It happened frequently that the company's district managers—Esmerelda's bosses—came by to ensure that the employees were performing to corporate standards. Sometimes these managers announced themselves, but other times, they showed up incognito as secret shoppers (a phrase that still strikes fear in my heart a decade later). While these visits didn't mean Esmerelda's job was on the line, her employees' jobs definitely were. Some had actually been fired because, despite Esmerelda's exacting standards and watchful eye, they were not performing up to snuff when the district manager came around. Esmerelda had seen people lose their jobs—which, for some employees, meant losing their livelihood—and so she continued to comment, judge, and berate in an effort to help us avoid a similar fate.

You may be surprised to hear this, but instead of tuning out Esmerelda's voice, I listened. After a particularly scary experience with a secret shopper who pretended to be an irate customer (I mean, does it *really* need to get this deep?) I found myself thanking Esmerelda for looking out for me. I remember thinking what a turning point this would be in our relationship—me expressing my sincere appreciation to Esmerelda in such a mature and evolved way, her responding with teary-eyed gratitude for finally being seen by her young protégé.

Of course, it didn't happen this way. I did express some thanks, but Esmerelda was a little leery of my gratitude—not unfair, considering I had been pretty cold toward her for months prior. However, I continued listening to her comments and let her know I appreciated what she shared (even when I didn't always do what she asked). Over time, it seemed like she could be more relaxed around me as well, because she knew I paid attention to her critiques when I needed to, and that otherwise, I could handle things on my own.

If you are getting the idea that this is the kind of relationship I am suggesting you create with your inner critic, you are spot on.

What if this part of you is actually on your side?

What if its judgy comments aren't coming from a sadistic desire to watch you suffer, but rather from worry that if you step out of line, you may get hurt?

What if this part of you developed when you were a kid because it saw that people did not always respond to your needs if you didn't seem pleasant or compliant or good enough?

What if this part of you would love to rest and maybe have a better relationship with you, but is terrified of what will happen if it stops doing its job for even a moment?

Your relationship with your "manager" part has been strained for so long. You've gotten used to hating it, resenting it, blaming it for your sadness, worry, and low self-esteem. The more resentful you get, the more convinced your manager becomes that you need them—clearly, it reasons, you need it to ensure that your messy emotions don't get in the way of you getting your needs met.

When we hate, resent, and blame our manager, we ignore the potentially useful things it has to share with us. At this moment, my manager is actually helping me write this chapter, coaching me about how the reader will perceive the words on the page, reminding me to pay attention to little details like grammar and sentence structure. These comments are necessary so this book provides an organized and coherent narrative versus a random assortment of my internal musings such as, *Why do people send eight separate text messages at once instead of one message?* or *Are Pop-Tarts really pastries? Because I miss them.*

To be clear, I am not saying it's beneficial to hear internal critiques and self-judgments played on "repeat." What *is* helpful is changing our relationship with this part of ourselves so that it doesn't need to get so loud, and so mean, for us to pay attention to it. When we let our manager know that we are paying attention, the manager can relax, and maybe even have some fun with us. It will still let us know what needs to get done—that is a manager's job, after all—but their comments will become more constructive, supporting us in becoming the high-achieving badasses we are, and making room for all of the easier-to-love parts of us to have their moment in the driver's seat. While there may be the occasional tug-of-war for attention, all of our parts will learn that we appreciate them for the function they serve in our lives.

Side note: Thank you, Esmerelda, for always looking out for me in the only way you know how, and for heart-ing my Instagram post about Pop-Tarts that one time.

As you may have guessed, learning to love all parts of yourself is not as easy as gaining a chapter's worth of insight and doing a single exercise. The work of self-love is a lifelong commitment, requiring repeated effort and continuous practice. There are times when it will seem like your parts are all working in harmony—I am having moments while writing this book when my creative, imaginative, organizing, and structured parts all work together, and my hands fly over the keyboard. In other moments, my inner Esmerelda gets loud as hell when I get stuck thinking, *No one is going to like this,* or *This makes no sense,* or *What if I do all of this work and no one cares?*

That's when I have to thank Esmerelda for her thoughts, let her know I'm listening, and invite one of my other parts join the conversation. Every conversation has enough room for everyone to be heard.

MANAGER MEET AND GREET

By now, you are probably thinking about your own inner critic/manager/Esmerelda. In the space below, draw a picture of this part of you. There are no guidelines for what this picture needs to include or how big or how small it should be—just draw whatever comes to mind.

Now that you've visualized this part of you, ask your manager the following questions, and journal your responses below.

- What is your hope for me?
- How are you trying to help me?
- When did you first start showing up?
- What would you be doing if it wasn't this?
- Anything else you want to tell me?

Thank your manager for sharing whatever was shared, and write any additional reflections below.

Self-Care

Merriam-Webster Dictionary: *Care for oneself; specifically: health care provided by oneself often without the consultation of a medical professional.*

Urban Dictionary: *Self-care is an umbrella term that Twitter/Tumblr SJWs use to excuse their poor financial decisions. Why spend money on things like rent/bills when you can buy coloring books from Whole Foods?*

I'm six months behind on rent, my phone got shut off, and my cars getting repo'd. I'm going to a $400 spa though because self-care.

APA Dictionary of Psychology: *Self-care has been defined as providing adequate attention to one's own physical and psychological wellness (Beauchamp & Childress, 2001).*

2

SELF-CARE

If you need something entertaining to do on a Monday evening, try searching "#selfcare" on Instagram. Among the 68 million hits you may find (this search is second only to #selflove, which had 95 million hits) will be posts such as these:

- "What triggers you is a reflection of your healing."
- "You are allowed to change the price of what it costs to access you."
- "Don't fill your cup just so you can serve others. Fill it simply because you are worthy of being filled."
- "Choose people who choose you."

Each of these posts certainly have more than a grain of truth in them; I can even see myself mentioning some of them in therapy. The challenge is how broad and sometimes tangential they are. Just like the self-love content we talked about in the introduction, these posts are certainly related to self-care, but ultimately make the real definition more elusive.

If the sheer number of hits doesn't convince you, Google Trends analytics illustrate that the topic of self-care is a widely-researched term. While many related words have seasonal peaks and dips in popularity (Valentine's Day really drives interest in self-work), self-care remains as steady as a rock, with a consistently high number of worldwide searches. Clearly, just as with self-love, we want to understand what it really means.

Luckily, we've got a plethora of platforms to research these answers on a leisurely Monday evening. Move on to Twitter and you'll find #selfcare posts such as "Self-Care Saturday" accompanied by what looks like a dog enjoying a luxurious spa day (he totally deserves that), and of course "Self-Care Sunday," illustrated by a group of friends enjoying the hallowed weekend tradition of day-drinking their way through different bars and restaurants. And because it's social media, you'll also find a number of sponsored posts within your #selfcare search, including the "Thank God It's Thursday" campaign from the ABC network, which encourages viewers (female viewers specifically) to get their self-care in the form of binge-watching TV drama series.

Don't get me wrong, I'm all about these designated days and their catchy names. I love looking at people's luxurious spa visits and learning about, for example, the turtle-racing bar with bottomless mimosas. I'm also a lifelong *Grey's Anatomy* fan, so you know I'm tuning in for #TGIT on the weekly. Still, are any of these activities *really* self-care? Just how much has the definition of self-care been overhauled by marketing and consumerism?

When Self-Care and Consumerism Meet

Remember that *Urban Dictionary* definition of self-care? No need to flip the pages back—I'll remind you: "an excuse for poor financial decisions." Yes, I'm aware that *Urban Dictionary* is more like *Wikipedia's* sassy cousin than a scientifically grounded source of information. Yet even this snarky definition has a kernel of truth we should pay attention to, one that accurately portrays how self-care is often perceived. This perception isn't surprising, considering how prolific the self-care industry has become, particularly since the COVID-19 pandemic. Capitalism heard our cries for help and responded with self-care teas, self-care soaps, self-care popcorn . . . the list goes on and on.

Dissenters to this industry argue that capitalism itself creates the need for self-care in the first place, increasing its demands on the labor force and then offering a "solution" in the form of ridiculously expensive self-care products. While I don't know enough to make a cogent argument for or against that theory, I do know that self-care can't be boiled down to products, hashtags, or witty remarks on *Wikipedia's* outcast cousin. The proof can be found in self-care's origin story.

The Feminist Roots of Self-Care

Far from the boardroom of a marketing agency or the laboratory of a psychological research team, the roots of self-care can be traced to social activism—specifically, radical feminist groups in the 1950s who were resisting systems of patriarchy, white supremacy, and capitalism. These activists found that their work could be so mentally and physically draining that an intentional focus on self-care was needed to keep their powerful movements alive.

Well, damn. I don't know about you, but that history helps me grasp how empowering, transformative, and ultimately life-changing and history-making developing healthy self-care can be for us. It tells me self-care can serve as the vehicle we need to sustain the movements, actions, beliefs, and values that are most central to our being. It also tells me that neglecting self-care can make us so burned out and overwhelmed that we no longer have the energy, let alone the desire, to pursue the things we care about most.

It's interesting to note that self-care as we know it began with badass women claiming the time to nurture themselves to sustain their legacy work, yet it's the same type of badass women who are the main target for all that tea, soap, and popcorn. As I said, I'm not here to make an argument about consumerism, but rather to understand how the definition of self-care has been particularly distorted for women. So let's break it down.

A Self-Care Breakdown

As mentioned previously, self-care is an umbrella term that encompasses any actions we take to enhance our life and health as a protective measure against stress, burnout, and poor mental health. As you can imagine, given the popularity and ubiquity of self-care, numerous studies aim at identifying the main components of self-care. Lisa Butler's (2019) self-care model is particularly compelling as she and her coauthors cite and describe six major domains of self-care in order of importance: physical, professional, relational, emotional, psychological, and spiritual (Butler, et al., 2019).

The Physical Domain

The physical domain involves tending to the needs of the physical body, particularly essentials like restful sleep, proper nutrition, and getting enough exercise. I don't know about y'all, but I can already spot one out of these three that I could certainly be getting a little more of in my life. But one more aspect of the physical domain that often goes missed is preventive healthcare, such as going for your annual well woman exam or getting annual physicals. (Hopefully you're not like me, finding any excuse I can to put off my annual doctor appointments. *Hmmm, traffic will likely be bad at 2:00 p.m. on a Wednesday—better put it off till they open those evening appointments. See you next year, Dr. Danzinger!*)

I want to acknowledge my privilege as a healthy, able-bodied person who can make the casual choice to avoid doctor's appointments. It is just this kind of privilege that encourages us to be so cavalier with our health. We will move mountains to ensure we don't miss the latest episode of our favorite prestige drama, to make it to girls' night at Postino's for that $20-bottle-and-bruschetta special, and certainly to finish that work project by deadline, yet we drag our feet when it comes to our physical health unless (or until) something is seriously wrong.

I could try to make a strong argument on the importance of tending to your health, not only so that you feel fit for all your daily badassery, but I'm not going to—many great books lay out all the reasons why and how tending to your physical health helps you live longer and better. What I will tell you is why the physical domain of self-care is listed first: the physical domain is the foundational piece of self-care that ensures all the other pieces can exist.

Maybe your nutrition is good and you're in Pilates class three times a week, but your sleep has been going downhill for years, and you've canceled on your doctor so often that the receptionist has your name on an "Annoying Patients" list. (I really believe they have those.) If this is the case, I challenge you right now to think of one thing, just one tiny thing, you could start doing to improve your physical self-care. Maybe go on a walk with your dog in the morning instead of just letting them out in the yard, or maybe schedule a dentist appointment without waiting for tooth pain to make it for you. Self-care comes down to choices, so make the choice to care about your health enough to do something.

The Professional Domain

As I mentioned, the order of these domains is intentional within the Butler model. When I saw that the professional domain came right after physical, a large part of me resisted this idea. Like many others, as much I love my work, I often try to diminish the amount of time and space it takes up in my life. Still, I can't argue that our work does take a significant portion of our lives—in the US, we spend approximately a third of our time at work or engaged in work-related tasks (Giuntella, et al., 2021).

This reality makes it all the more important that we give ourselves top-notch professional self-care. At its most basic, this means taking measures to manage the stress that comes with your job. Knowing how easily work can blur into the edges of other parts of your life, this could look like putting boundaries in place to protect how much energy you give to your job. It could also mean tiny but impactful acts like listening to a meditation on your drive home from work to help you wind down.

Based on personal experience, I strongly recommend taking the time to consider what a healthy wind-down ritual from work could be for you. If not a meditation, perhaps try a soothing playlist or a standing phone date with a friend.

Another part of professional self-care that I love is taking proactive steps to enhance job satisfaction and performance. This could look like finding a mentor or personal coach or seeking out trainings that improve your skill set while also offering intellectual stimulation. On the flip side, professional self-care could mean taking more intangible (but just as impactful) steps to change your mindset about work and what it means to you.

Many clients I work with tell me they just want work to be something they do to make money. I support this mindset 100 percent, if it works for them. Unfortunately, for the vast majority of folks I see, it doesn't. Even those who tell me they don't care about work spend 90 percent of their session talking about it—how what they do doesn't matter or how stupid their coworkers/boss/projects are. These people's professional self-care task is to accept that work doesn't need to be a shining positive in their life, but taking control of how they think about it can save them *so* much energy, give them greater professional satisfaction, and even improve their performance.

The Relational Domain

Next comes the relational domain of self-care, which involves efforts to create, nurture, and maintain our relationships. Relational self-care could take the form of seeking and creating new relationships or regularly checking in and connecting with your existing social networks. Sounds simple enough, right? Nevertheless, one of my most common refrains in therapy is, "We suck at friendships as adults."

Sound like overgeneralizing? Consider that access to friends is almost guaranteed through school, college, and early jobs—environments where we are usually surrounded by similarly aged peers. But once we reach our mid-twenties, access to friends is much less guaranteed. We may be careful to not become too close to our coworkers due to professional boundaries, or just because we spend enough time with our coworkers and would like some variety outside of work. Another factor is the rise of remote work, which can decrease access to work friends. Instead, we find friends at "extracurricular" activities: the gym, parenting groups, or that pottery class. Still, you may find making friends harder without, for instance, a teacher forcing you to work in groups. Instead, you may have to vet the room for friend potential, introduce yourself to a total rando, and hope something sticks. That's not easy!

Whether you take the initiative to make new friends or have some old friends from your school days who have made it all the way to adulthood with you, you must still clear the second barrier to adult friendships: keeping them alive. I often hear clients, as well as my own friends, complain, "I invite my friends so much, but they flake," or else, "I want to spend time with my friends, but I always have so much going on."

Both statements feel very true for many of us. We've all been the flaky friend at times—hey, we *do* have a lot going on, from work to caretaking (spouses, kids, extended family, and fur babies) to "me time." We've also been the one seeking out connection with others and hearing back, "Oooh, I *want* to, but work has been so busy lately . . . I think I'm just going to stay in tonight." It takes energy to invite friends to do things together, *and* it takes energy to accept invitations. A friend recently told me about a last-minute trip she took with four other women; what struck me the most was not the amazing spontaneity of this adventure, but the fact that five adults could manage the logistical gymnastics of coordinating schedules to go on a trip.

The multiple challenges inherent to adult friendships makes it even more important to be proactive and thoughtful in the way we create and maintain relationships. We have hacks, shortcuts, and time-management strategies for so many parts of our lives, but we rarely use them when it comes to our friendships. I get that it feels weird to, say, set a reminder to text your friends once a week; still, if we care enough about our health to set a reminder for spin class, why don't we prioritize our friendships to the same degree? So consider how you could make your relational self-care just a little easier. Maybe set a reminder to check in with your besties, or maybe initiate a monthly first Sunday hang so your crew doesn't have to perform schedule gymnastics each month.

These steps, shortcuts, and scheduling strategies will save you precious time and energy and, just as importantly, they will ensure that you have consistent access to a vital component of self-care—your relationships. I've said it before, and I will likely say it about thirteen more times, we are wired for connection. Growth, healing, and learning cannot exist solely in isolation. Thus, taking time to nurture and maintain relationships allows us to give back to ourself and sustain the amazing growth work we've been working toward. Also, turtle racing is best enjoyed with good company!

The Emotional Domain

The emotional domain of self-care involves management of your emotional experiences in an effort to enhance the positive experiences and to minimize *prolonged* negative experiences. I emphasize "prolonged" because negative emotional experiences—anxiety, worry, anger, sadness, stress—are normative to the human experience. In fact, as most people have likely experienced, many things you love and enjoy most can include challenging emotions from time to time. For instance, I love making LEGO flower bouquets—yes, this is a thing—because it brings me a sense of accomplishment, joy, and peace; sometimes it also brings frustration, discouragement, and occasional financial anxiety. My LEGO bonsai tree is definitely not constructed correctly, and I will probably never fix it.

However, there is a point where our negative emotional experiences can become so prolonged that we find ourselves stuck in a negative loop. Like quicksand, the more we struggle, the more we sink—in other words, we feel like shit about feeling like shit. This is where emotional self-care comes into play. It starts with the development of healthy coping skills such as meditating, journaling regularly, and engaging in hobbies that provide a sense of mastery. It also means taking the time to identify what coping skills you've been using that are not working. For instance, maybe watching Netflix has been a go-to coping skill over the past couple years, but do you want it to be? Do you notice it being helpful to you? And if so, is it helpful in the long run or just in the moment?

In developing your emotional domain, it's important to understand the difference between self-care and self-soothing. While self-care is aimed at creating long-term improvement in multiple domains of your life, self-soothing involves actions that temporarily alleviate your distress.

Self-soothing is incredibly adaptive—I remember marveling at my daughter's ability to calm herself down by sucking on her thumb—but while it can provide a short burst of relief when needed, it will not contribute to sustained emotional health. Real emotional self-care utilizes skills that help you acknowledge and manage your emotional experience. (Note that I again used the word *manage,* not *reduce.* While a reduction of negative emotions may sometimes result, the real purpose of self-care is to support you in managing the intensity of these emotions.)

I often describe the management of emotional experiences with the analogy of a radio. Think of a really annoying song that you absolutely hate. (Right now, mine is "Marry You." I love Bruno Mars, but his songs are *so* overplayed.) Now imagine yourself trapped in a rideshare with that song on repeat. While you can't turn off the song, you can manage your experience by doing things such as looking out the window at the scenery or talking to a friend sitting beside you who agrees that this song sucks. All of a sudden you realize the song has gotten a little quieter in your mind—instead of "I think I wanna marry you" running through your brain, you are thinking about how much you appreciate your friend and her great taste in music. Conversely, if you love the song that is playing, you'll want to turn up the volume, roll down the windows, scream-sing at the top of your lungs—in other words, pay as much attention to enjoying it as possible. (For me, there's no better scream-sing option right now than "Incomplete" by Backstreet Boys.)

In the same way, we can't always turn an emotional experience off or on, but there are things we can do to amplify or minimize its volume. And while there are a lot of self-care tips around managing the intensity of our negative emotional experiences, amplifying our positive emotional experiences by leaning into an experience, naming it, and sharing our gratitude for it is an aspect of self-care that often gets missed.

Take the time to consider something you truly love and enjoy in your life, and brainstorm one thing you could do to turn that radio knob up a notch. Could you connect with someone else over your shared joy, or add or change something in your environment to make the emotional experience a little bit better? Practicing this skill of amplification can lead to increased life satisfaction and, a bonus: learning to work with your more enjoyable emotions also better equips you to minimize the emotions that may feel a little too loud.

Personally, I've resolved that I will not only listen to "Incomplete" at max volume, but I will regularly listen to it in my living room, so I have lots of dancing room and a remote handy to use as my mic. Cheesy? Yes. Incredibly satisfying and fun? Also yes.

The Psychological and Spiritual Domains

While each of these domains are powerful and meaningful in their own right, I've combined them here because they can overlap. Both domains of self-care refer to the steps we take to satisfy curiosity, experience fulfillment, and live a meaningful life aligned with our values. Thus, psychological or spiritual self-care can take the form of intellectually stimulating activities such as engaging in courses or trainings, reading thought-provoking books (such as this one), or engaging in novel activities like playing the drums or skydiving. If you happen to be a professional skydiver, maybe consider taking up crossword puzzles. Sky's the limit here (yep, had to do it).

This domain can also involve participating in religious or faith-based communities, or seeking alternative spiritual avenues based on mindfulness and connection with nature. The beautiful thing about these domains is that there is no "right" way to approach them—each of us will have different "recipes" to achieve psychological and spiritual fulfillment.

Ongoing examination, exploration, and experimentation is vital in all the domains of self-care, but especially in the psychological and spiritual domains. While one activity or mindset may serve you at a certain juncture, most people will likely reach a point when they need to evolve or change what they're doing to adapt to a new situation or need in life. One beautiful way to explore your changing needs is with an activity that, in my workplace, is known as "signing up for life classes." Remember how you could audit classes back in college? If there was something you were interested in, you could "sit in" on the class with no strings attached. This system allowed you to listen to a philosophy lecture or participate in a chemistry lab while still having the freedom to opt out and try something else if you got bored. The same type of opportunity is available through "life classes" offered through community centers, libraries, churches, and yes, local colleges and trade schools.

The beauty of this exercise is the freedom it offers to bring novelty and intellectual stimulation into your life, as well as the possibility of connecting with meaningful hobbies, enriching organizations, or even just new friends. Consider what life classes you might want to sign up for in the next year. Maybe improve your knife skills as an amateur chef, seek your Financial Analyst certification, or take a weekend course in something you know you'll never stick to but have always wondered about. The goal in this domain is not mastery or even achievement; rather, it's about taking the time to nurture your psychological and spiritual parts, which allows for a deeper sense of meaning, fulfillment, and purpose in your life.

Five Impactful Ways to Start Improving Your Self-Care

My first draft of this section had the title "Five *Quick* Ways," but as you will come to see, while the actions themselves may feel quick, the stress you have to tolerate in doing them, the energy you need to maintain them, and the resilience you will build as you continue doing them (especially when life gets hard) are anything but quick to develop. Self-care doesn't lend itself to quick and dirty tricks, alas. However, I can provide some impactful steps to begin improving your self-care across all domains.

These little tips were woven through the previous sections, but if you are anything like me, you skimmed right past them without pausing to engage. So let's take the time to pause and explore how you can begin improving your self-care today.

1. **Physical Domain:** What is one small, tangible thing you could introduce this week that would improve your sleep, nutrition, or body movement?
2. **Professional Domain:** Consider how/if you do anything to wind down after work. What could you do differently to help you transition from work to home life? (If you are not currently working, consider how you could wind down from any transition you experience in your day such as when your child goes down for the night, or after you get home from running errands).
3. **Relational Domain:** Think of one time-management strategy you use in your life to make the most of your energy (i.e., reminders, smartphone apps, a calendar diary). What is one way you could utilize your existing

time-management strategies to better maintain your relationships?

4. **Emotional Domain:** Consider one aspect of your life that you deeply enjoy, from your favorite hobby to your favorite people. Choose one thing you could do to immerse yourself in this experience a little more deeply.
5. **Psychological and Spiritual Domains:** As you reflect on what topics or practices interest or challenge you, identify at least two life classes you want to sign up for in the next year.

If, like me, you are an eager beaver when it comes to self-improvement, you may have already started to formulate responses to each of these steps. YAY! I bet it feels amazing. I also bet that you have a busy life with many things to manage simultaneously. While introducing new self-care techniques can be a major catalyst for growth, it's important to pace yourself, knowing how much you are already carrying. For now, choose just one of these domains to begin working on, then make the choice to keep trying, keep experimenting, and keep evolving your self-care. You are worth it.

Self-Trust

Merriam-Webster Dictionary: *Great faith in oneself or one's abilities.*

Urban Dictionary: *One who believes in his or her capabilities, one who is confident enough to handle life efficiently.*

APA Dictionary of Psychology: *Trust in one's abilities, capacities, and judgment.*

3

SELF-TRUST

If we consult the social media sphere for a definition of self-trust, the lack of chatter is both shocking and telling. Where #selfcare yields an immense 68 million Instagram hits and #selfesteem brings a respectable 3 million, #selftrust comes in at a barely detectable 175 thousand hits. This isn't surprising, given that the concept of self-trust is not widely known or even discussed outside the therapeutic or coaching sphere. In fact, of the few posts I see, the majority came from therapists and coaches. On the upside, this means less misinformation and confusion being spread about the topic. Of course, we do have a few outliers included within the tag, such as:

- "Things I hate include phone calls, small talk, ticking clocks, and ambiguity."
- "It's time to get SOUL naked."
- "My mind is like an internet browser: nineteen tabs open, three of them are frozen, and I have no idea where the music is coming from."

Yep, that clears up . . . nothing. While each of these posts may contain commentary on someone's internal experience, the concept remains unclear to the audience, and, I predict, even to the people who created the posts. They are not alone. Even among mental health professionals, this concept is not a ubiquitous one (certainly not in the way self-care or self-love is), but it is certainly an essential one. Let's explore what it looks like in practice.

Do You Trust Yourself?

Vanessa is a successful lawyer who is feeling that heady combination of excited, nervous, and "WTF am I doing?!" as she prepares to move in with her boyfriend. One of her dominant concerns is that she has made wonderful progress in carving out time for herself—something she deeply needs as a staunch introvert, but which is not easy to do in her incredibly demanding industry. She has found this solo time essential to maintaining her mental health, keeping her energized, and helping her continue to be a formidable lawyer while sustaining a healthy, growing relationship. After working hard to maintain boundaries around her time, she fears that once she moves in with her more extroverted boyfriend, she will not be able to keep that time for herself.

Listening to Vanessa's concerns, I feel how pivotal a moment this is for her. I witnessed the moment she realized that taking time for herself was not just a luxury, but a truly foundational pillar to her well-being. I supported her as she took each challenging step to carve out this solo time in an already packed schedule and had a front-row seat for the transformation she experienced in making this time a priority as non-negotiable as the items on her work agenda.

Now as Vanessa talks through the fears she has around balancing her boyfriend's needs with her deep desire for daily solitude, I gently interrupt: "Do you trust yourself?"

Vanessa pauses, taken off guard. "What do you mean?" she asks, confused but already a little intrigued.

"I mean do you trust yourself—the future you—to figure this out?"

Defining Self-Trust

Self-trust can be broken down into two parts:

1. Truly believing in your competency.
2. Being reliable enough with yourself that you can depend on this competency.

Based on our many months working together, Vanessa and I both know she has the capacity to carve out time for herself—she doesn't need help with the how. I ask Vanessa if she feels capable of communicating with her boyfriend about the boundaries she needs. Fortunately, her answer to this is a resounding yes. We also explore whether she can trust future Vanessa to handle any future boundary challenges she may face. Again, a resounding yes.

My next question is where things could get tricky. I ask Vanessa, "Do you trust yourself to *maintain* these boundaries when it gets hard?"

Vanessa thinks for a moment, and her eyes fill as she softly responds, "I guess I don't. I don't trust myself to show up for me."

Damn, that hurts to hear, and I know it hurt for Vanessa to say. It hurts because trust is something we need and depend on to feel safe in a relationship. Thus, if I acknowledge that I don't trust myself, I then acknowledge that I don't feel safe in my relationship with myself. That can be deeply unsettling and destabilizing.

Are You a Flaky Friend . . . to Yourself?

Like self-love, self-trust is not automatic. Just as in any relationship, self-trust needs to be developed and nurtured, and it can be damaged if there are enough ruptures. Recall that there are two parts to self-trust: truly believing in your competency *and* being reliable enough with yourself that you can depend on this competency. While I may genuinely feel competent to do what I need, I can only fully trust myself if I also depend on myself to consistently exercise that competency when I need it. But what if that's not the case? What if, when I recall my history, it's littered by instances in which I made a commitment to myself and broke it, or intentionally committed to something that I knew I didn't want? Well, that's when . . .

When you hear the term "flaky friend," you know instantly what it means: someone you enjoy being with and maybe truly love, but whom you know is completely unreliable. You may even have someone immediately come to mind—let's call her Lola. If you make a plan with Lola, you know the odds are about 50–50 that it will actually happen. Being the fun-loving and agreeable gal she is, Lola says yes to pretty much everything you ask of her, but when the day comes, she has all the excuses in the world, from the reasonable (her car is in the shop, and Uber is so expensive during this surge time) to the flimsy (she's not feeling well) to the questionable (her dog isn't feeling well—maybe what she had was contagious?).

When you think of Lola, you may have mixed feelings. On one hand, when she does show up, she is warm, fun to be around, and has a sarcastic edge that keeps you cackling. You often leave your hangouts feeling energized and restored, and even find yourself chuckling a couple of days later, remembering that hilarious bit Lola did about PopSockets. (Google it.) But then there's the other 50 percent of the time, when she's MIA because of another lame excuse. Over time, you find that you reach out to Lola less and less, not because you don't love spending time with her, but because you've learned not to trust her when she makes a commitment to you. After a while, even though you truly love and care about Lola, you stop reaching out to her because it is more painful to count on someone so inconsistent than to just give up the relationship.

Lola isn't flaky because she is malicious or lazy or doesn't give a shit about you. The problem is that Lola has been conditioned since an early age to betray her own trust, which makes her untrustworthy even to people she cares about and who care about her.

By now, you've probably guessed where I'm going: our tendency, especially as women, to become Lolas to ourselves.

When we are present with ourselves, we are vibrant, loving, a joy to be around. But when we are inconsistent with ourselves, we become Lola. We make promises to ourselves, but then forget them the minute something or someone else comes up. We commit to take action on our own behalf, but when the moment comes, we decide it doesn't really matter all that much. We say yes to something that feels meaningful or important, but subconsciously know there is no way we will actually follow through. This is how self-trust breaks down before it even has a chance to build.

Women, Your Self-Trust Will be Tested

As women, our competency is questioned in many ways, implicit and explicit, subtle and overt. For example, numerous studies have found that resumes with names that appear to belong to women or minorities are routinely chosen less often than those with names that sound white and male (Parasurama, Sedoc, & Ghose, 2022). Our competency is questioned before we even get our foot in the door. Additionally, women are given far fewer opportunities when it comes to leadership positions. Lean In (2021), an organization dedicated to helping women of all identities achieve their ambitions, found that since 2016, for every 100 men hired to a manager position, only 86 women are hired to a similar position.

Additionally, much of the work women do goes unnoticed. For instance, women often provide much more emotional support, mentoring, and recruitment of underrepresented individuals than their male counterparts. This kind of work, though essential to the success and longevity of a company, often goes unseen and unacknowledged.

Even if you have full confidence in your abilities, these kinds of systemic prejudices may impact how you evaluate your sense of competency. I recommend a wonderful article from the *Harvard Business Review* called "Stop Telling Women They Have Imposter Syndrome" (Tulshyan & Burey, 2022). I mean, the title alone says it all, right? This article suggests that the disparity in opportunities and treatment between women of color and their white cisgender male counterparts has as much to do with their environment as the women's beliefs about their own competency.

While there have been some hopeful advancements in correcting the gender gap (as well as the many other bias-based gaps), there is something empowering about recognizing the context for our problem with self-trust. I'll show you what I mean by returning to Vanessa.

I can tell Vanessa is about to fall into a shame spiral, believing that not trusting herself must mean something is deeply wrong with her. Before she goes there, we explore other possibilities: her self-trust issue might have something to do with not keeping promises to herself, but having her competency questioned again and again in the male-dominated law industry certainly hasn't helped. This is not intended to absolve Vanessa of responsibility for repairing her self-trust; rather, it's meant to help Vanessa gain a realistic idea of all the ways her self-trust is being eroded so she can better defend herself from it. As we say in the therapy world, "Once you can name it, you can tame it." As Vanessa is more able to name the implied attacks on her competency, she'll become more capable of resisting those attacks and rebuilding her self-trust.

Of course, the attacks on our self-trust don't only come from the outside. I may believe I am capable of something, but can I count on myself to show up for me when I need to? All of us can struggle with this, but women in particular may struggle to be reliable to themselves. Countless studies have shown that in dual-income heterosexual households, women take the lion's share of household work (Cerrato & Cifre, 2018). This only increases when kids enter the picture, regardless of who is the primary breadwinner. Additionally, women have been found to bear the brunt of the emotional labor in the family, from initiating important conversations to maintaining relationships to finding opportunities for their family members' personal growth. Amid work priorities, household management, emotional maintenance, and social coordination, our personal needs tend to end up dead last on the priority list (assuming they get a space on the list at all). If we continually abandon our promises to ourselves because there is always something else that society/our boss/our partner says is more important, it's no wonder our self-trust has taken a hit.

This idea—that the needs of others are more important than what we want or need—is often reinforced as early as childhood. Imagine that you are a little girl, maybe six years old, and your grandmother has come to visit. You haven't seen her in weeks (which is essentially years in child time) and you are understandably a little cautious. Your parents encourage you to go give Grandma a hug and kiss. You shake your head—you know what you want at this moment, and it's not to hug the semi-stranger in front of you. Your parents say, "Be a good girl. Grandma came all this way to see you!" After much cajoling and scolding from your parents, you realize that communicating your desires only makes everyone more upset—at that point, you relent and give your grandma a hug and kiss, even though you did not want to. While this may seem like a minor occurrence in the grand scheme of childhood, something deeper is playing out in this interaction. Being encouraged to ignore our intuition or abandon our needs in favor of prioritizing the needs of others teaches us the "value" of betraying our self-trust. (Seeing our mothers do the same thing—saying no to themselves to say yes to others—only reinforces the habit further.)

We need to get into a habit of saying yes to ourselves. I don't mean saying yes to each desire, urge, or whim suggested by your id (the pleasure-seeking part of you); what I do mean is getting in the habit of saying yes to the commitments we make to ourselves. Think of people and things you are already in a habit of saying yes to—perhaps your boss, your clients, your parents, your favorite television show. (I am definitely an easy yes to watching *Insecure* every Monday evening.) There's good news here: you are already good at saying yes to things! It's just a matter of exercising that same consistency with yourself.

The Formula for Self-Trust

I wish I could give you a simple formula for self-trust, like loudly declaring, "I trust you," a certain number of times or overcoming a monumental barrier that proves your competency in front of everyone who doubted you. But alas, the reality is that self-trust comes down to the same practices that build trust in all our important relationships: consistency, doing the hard work, and doing more hard work when we eff things up (and we will all eff things up eventually).

To start, consider specific, concrete commitments you want to make to yourself—the more detailed, the better. For example, committing to "go outside more" is great, but so vague that it could be considered fulfilled by that walk you took from your parking spot to your office; instead, make your commitments short and specific, such as "I will go outside every three hours for five minutes" or "I will go for one twenty-minute walk at the end of the day."

Take a moment to make a commitment to yourself for the next week, then write it out in the space below.

Exercise

I commit to: *(Example)* go outside every three hours for at least five minutes.

I commit to: ______________________________

____

____

____

____

> Notice that I said "commitment" instead of "commitments." While I'm all about aiming high, allow yourself to start slowly here. The road to rebuilding self-trust is a long one, and success is measured in the quality of how you keep these commitments versus the number of commitments you can create.

Now let's say you have all the intentions in the world to follow through on this important commitment to yourself. But then, good old Lola shows up with lots of excuses—"I couldn't go outside because it was raining, and I forgot my umbrella," or "I couldn't go outside because my boss was in town, and he is militant about us staying on task," or "I couldn't go outside because I totally forgot I wrote down that commitment last week." Lola, you can be so predictable sometimes!

This is where repair becomes essential. When we notice how we failed to keep a commitment to ourselves, the typical response is to beat ourselves up about it for a minute (or more), then move on to the next item on our to-do list. This pattern reinforces that we are not very reliable and that self-trust is not all that important anyway.

For that reason, while I know you will be keeping the wonderful commitment to yourself that you just wrote down, on the off chance that life (or Lola) gets in the way, take a moment to complete the following prompts.

Exercise

I made a commitment to: *(Example)* go outside every three hours for at least five minutes.

My action on this commitment looked like: *(Example)* going one time on Monday and then moving it to the bottom of my priority list.

What I want to do next time is: *(Example)* set an alarm on my watch to remind me to go outside.

I made a commitment to: ______________________

My action on this commitment looked like: ______________________

What I want to do next time is: ______________________

As you may note, the wording in this exercise is intentionally designed not to shame you for breaking your commitment. Experience tells me that if you didn't complete it, it wasn't because you're lazy or just don't give a fuck. Instead, it's likely something else became more important and deprioritized your commitment. It happens! But by taking the time to repair and plan for the future, you are reaffirming that your self-trust matters, making it more likely that you will be successful in keeping your commitment in the future.

I mean, imagine if Lola did that! Let's say you wake up the morning after she flaked on you (again) and find a text saying, "Dude, my bad for bailing yesterday. Hanging out with you is really important to me, so I'm going to make it happen if you will let me. How about I meet you outside your work at the end of the day and we can walk to that ramen place? As an extra incentive, I have a funny PopSocket story just for you!"

Now, isn't Lola charming? She didn't just express regret for not keeping her commitment—she also conveyed how important her relationship with you is and how she wants to move toward repair. How can you resist patching things up with a friend like that? Except maybe you can—it's possible that you may still feel a little resistant, thinking of all the times you have been burned in the past. Fortunately, like you, Lola is committed to rebuilding your friendship by continuing to take the actions needed to maintain your trust. She knows that it won't just be about sending nice text messages after flaking—instead, it will be about her demonstrating again and again that she can be counted on. And if she does flake (remember, her dog is elderly and prone to illness), you know she will make a sincere effort to repair it with you. Similarly, even as you pledge to repairing your self-trust, you may experience moments of doubt or resistance as you feel resentful or helpless for the times you have let yourself down in the past or the inevitable times you will let yourself down again. Repairing self-trust is not about achieving a perfect track record with yourself; it's about consistently dedicating time, energy, and care toward yourself and taking the time to repair when mistakes happen.

We deserve this sincerity and consistency in all our relationships, especially ourselves, so let's begin rebuilding it.

Self-Control

Merriam-Webster Dictionary: *Restraint exercised over one's own impulses, emotions, or desires.*

Urban Dictionary: *One of the fruits of the Holy Spirit. A visible attribute of a true Christian life as found in Galatians 5:22–23.*

Having command or mastery over, or possession of, one's own behavior.

". . . make every effort to add to your faith, goodness; and to goodness, knowledge; and to knowledge, self-control; and to self-control, perseverance; and to perseverance, godliness; and to godliness, mutual affection; and to mutual affection, love." (NIV)

APA Dictionary of Psychology: *The ability to be in command of one's behavior (overt, covert, emotional, or physical) and to restrain or inhibit one's impulses. In circumstances in which short-term gain is pitted against long-term greater gain, self-control is the ability to opt for the long-term outcome.*

4

SELF-CONTROL

- "A person without self-control is like a city with broken-down walls."
- "Self-control begins with the mastery of our thoughts."
- "Self-control is strength."
- "Once you master detachment and self-control, nothing and no one can faze you."

Is it just me, or do these social media takes on self-control remind you of the definition of a robot? And not one of those cool robots that develops human-like emotions and ends up becoming besties with Will Smith, but one of those legit robots that just computes the functions you enter into it and is not affected by desires, wants, urges, or those pesky little things called feelings.

The concept of self-control cannot be fully understood without understanding the religious context in which it lives. The *Urban Dictionary* definition certainly makes this point, but the Bible is far from the only religion that teaches self-control as an essential virtue. While my intention with this chapter certainly isn't to question anyone's belief system or the meaningful role self-control may have in it, it's important to understand where your beliefs about this concept originated as we work to refine your relationship with it.

What Women Have Been Told About Self-Control

Let's begin by exploring what self-control means specifically as a woman. Research has shown that women exhibit greater impulse control and self-regulation than men, possibly due to a woman's biological need to be more selective than men in choosing mates (Chapple, et al., 2021). We can't just choose the first caveperson who walks into the clearing. If that research seems a little too tied to traditional gender stereotypes to be taken seriously, other studies posit that the consistently higher findings of self-control found in women could be due to social and gender influence.

Whatever the reason, women are often held to more stringent rules about the way they should control their bodies and manage their behavior starting from childhood, from ensuring they make no impolite noises ("A burp? God forbid!") to how they consume food ("Don't eat all of that cake! Control yourself.") to how they behave ("Look at Maya—such a good girl for waiting her turn. Jacob jumped the line, but boys will be boys."). Each of these examples reinforce the idea that girls need to be in control of their behaviors and, it follows, their emotions and desires.

By extension, a lapse in self-control for a man is perceived very differently than the same lapse for a woman. For example, if a man drops an accidental f-bomb during a job interview, his frankness is considered charming. If a woman does the exact same thing, hiring managers wonder about her professional decorum, which includes—yes—her capacity for self-control.

This difference has a dangerous impact when it comes to safety in heteronormative sexual dynamics. If women inherently have more self-control than men, as we're often told, it's up to us to put the brakes on a situation, since men are at the mercy of their physical desires. This assumption has so gotten into our heads as women over the millennia that it's been perpetuated. As a result, when we allow a breach in the self-control expected of us, we may experience deep shame within ourselves—*If I can't control myself, does that make me less of a good woman?*

As with many of the concepts in this book, the goal of this chapter is not to prescribe a certain dose of self-control you should have—I'm here for you having all the self-control you desire. The important word is YOU. I want you to feel empowered to act in a way that is congruent with your values and beliefs, rather than the agenda of some other person, ideology, or societal structure. In other words, a little less emphasis on the "control," and a little more on the "self."

Too Much of a "Good" Thing

Think of any person, place, or thing you enjoy. Maybe you picture your best friend, that beautiful lake near your house where all the ducks go to swim, or white chocolate mochas. (Those were oddly specific examples, I admit, but hold them in mind.) Now imagine if you had a shit ton of these available to you all the time. At first it would be great, but over time it could get a little overwhelming. Personally, I love hanging out with my bestie, but I need space to miss her. (And vice versa, I'm sure!) I love that lake, but wow, those ducks start to get on my nerves after too many visits in a row. And as much as I love the delicious richness of my favorite coffee drink, my stomach would definitely rebel against me for drinking it every single day.

You get the idea: there are so many things we love and value in the world, but any of them taken to excess can make us sick of them. Self-control is no exception to this rule, yet it doesn't stop our teachers from applauding our obedience, our coaches from praising our commitment, or social media from nagging us about healthy habits and behaviors, as if there were no downside to this extreme.

Despite what you may have heard, self-control is not a "one size fits all" category. You might benefit from learning to better regulate your emotions or adapt your behaviors so that you can reach your goals. Then again, you might have self-control coming out the wazoo and still find yourself unable to achieve those goals. Or maybe you don't find yourself fitting neatly into either category—some areas of your life could use more moderation and self-restraint, while other areas might benefit from a little push against the boundaries you've taken for granted. Finding your "size" requires you to learn what self-control means on *your* terms.

Grab your white chocolate mocha, and let's explore your relationship with self-control.

Introducing . . . the Overcontrolled Personality

Dialectical behavioral therapy (DBT; Linehan, 1993) was developed by Marsha Linehan to treat individuals with borderline personality disorder (BPD), a condition that causes chronic and persistent difficulties regulating emotions. DBT offers amazingly practical interventions for these individuals, such as progressive muscle relaxation, intense exercise, or even holding ice cubes in their hands. Even those without this diagnosis have found these interventions useful in moderating their emotional reactions.

Still, practitioners found that for some individuals seeking help with emotional regulation, even these well-known and research-backed DBT practices brought little to no benefit. Enter the overcontrolled (OC) personality type. The characteristics of this type—perfectionistic tendencies, emotional suppression and inhibition, elevated distress tolerance, high detail focus processing, and high threat sensitivity along with low reward responding—are collectively described as a pattern of "too much self-control." Turns out there really can be too much of a good thing.

Picture someone who has an impressive ability to delay gratification and a high desire to exceed expectations and perform well, someone who pays close attention to the most-minute details and holds the values of duty, responsibility, and fairness in the highest regard. Who comes to mind? Perhaps you are thinking of yourself (totally fine, if so) or maybe you are thinking of your high-achieving partner, your ultra-successful sister, or someone else equally badass. In the therapeutic context, we describe this as an *overcontrolled coping style*—a name that speaks to the inherent difficulties but not to the amazing benefits of living this way. Overcontrolled folks are the ones who will go the extra mile to ensure that that important project is not just completed but exceeds expectations. They are the party guests who come early and bring ice and your favorite type of cheese without having been asked. They're great to travel with because they've covered every contingency, from planning out your daily itinerary to booking the crazy early reservations. Bottom line, our overcontrolled folks keep the world turning!

However, overcontrolled coping has also been linked to feelings of social isolation, challenges in interpersonal relationships, hyper-perfectionism, rigidity, high risk aversion, and lack of emotional expression. These tendencies can contribute to the development of certain mental health conditions such as depression, anorexia nervosa, or obsessive-compulsive disorder. An additional challenge for our overcontrolled coping friends is that, on the surface, they seem as if they are doing just fine—thriving even! How could they not be, when they have it all together like that?

Yet beneath the surface, these individuals are often exhausted from the mental energy it takes to monitor every distracting impulse, emotion, or thought that goes through their mind. While their talent for structure and organization helps their lives function flawlessly, it comes at the price of spontaneity, flexibility, and openness. It's frequently said of overcontrolled coping that, if these folks were in a rose garden, they would mainly notice all the thorns and immediately begin formulating a plan to prevent anyone from getting poked. It's the perfect metaphor for high threat sensitivity ("This garden is dangerous—I see thorns everywhere I look") and low reward sensitivity ("There was a rose that smelled like white chocolate mocha? How did I miss that?")

Another problem for people who struggle with overcontrolled coping is the limited range of emotions they can express, ranging from polite smiles to a more stoic expression. This stunted emotional range can cause others to feel distant from them, but also give off the idea that they are fine and have no needs, vulnerabilities, or problems. I have a friend who leans this way; while her stoic exterior can lead to some hilariously dry delivery of sarcastic comments, it's also incredibly difficult to assess when she is upset unless you know the micro-behaviors that signal her distress, such as pulling her ear or a slight tightening of her jaw. This emotional opacity makes it difficult for folks who struggle with overcontrolled coping to get the support they need—even when they feel like their distress could not be more clear, all we see on the outside is the tiniest of ripples in an otherwise still pond.

In recent years, DBT therapists have adapted this form of therapy specifically to support folks with overcontrolled coping tendencies. In the process of developing this new approach, known as radically open DBT (RO-DBT; Hempel, et al., 2018), they found four core challenges that OC folks commonly experience:

1. **Low receptivity and openness.** Overcontrolled coping tends to come with a gift for pattern recognition and an amazing eye for detail; thus, more times than not, they may be able to quickly deduce the answers for any given problem or create a highly detailed and successful plan of attack for a dilemma. The drawback is that they may be so certain of their own ideas that they are resistant to feedback and struggle to play or work well with others.
2. **Low flexibility.** People struggling with overcontrolled coping need things to look a certain (read: predictable) way and have very established ideas about fairness and responsibility. Their moral compass isn't just strong; it's as rigid as if it were cast in concrete.
3. **Low emotional expressiveness or awareness.** As discussed above, the faces of people with overcontrolled coping tendencies often reflect only the subtlest changes in emotional expression, which can be off-putting and confusing to others. You invite them to a birthday party, expecting them to be excited, but their face resembles

the moment their boss announced nobody was getting bonuses that year.

4. **Challenges with social connection and intimacy.** Individuals who struggle with overcontrolled coping commonly describe feeling "different" and "apart" from others, and may often experience frustration in relationships (*Why do I have to remember everything? Why do I have to do everything? Why doesn't anyone ever get it right?*).

In my clinical practice, the majority of my clients are high-achieving professionals who are killing it at their careers, deeply committed to their relationships, listening to all the podcasts, and reading all the self-help books, yet they still find themselves struggling to manage their psychological well-being. One client in particular—let's call her Anja—is a skilled engineer, married to her wife of twelve years, and seems to be in a constant state of training for one endurance sport or another. Nevertheless, Anja struggles with moody "ups and downs" (mostly downs) and cannot figure out why. Even her certainty that she has everything she needs to be happy only serves to compound her "down" moments—she berates herself for being unhappy or unsatisfied for no reason.

Being the overachiever that she is, Anja attacks her mental health the same way she plans out her marathon training schedule. She does all the things recommended by self-help books and Dr. Google: she journals each night, meditates each morning, and even found dialectical behavioral therapy (DBT) worksheets to do when she feels upset. The woman is dedicated! But while these steps have had some positive impact on her life, Anja still feels no more capable of managing the lows than she was before.

When Anja brings in a spreadsheet in which she'd categorized her life into various health domains (physical, social, family, etc.), I have a pretty strong hunch that her personality might fall on the overcontrolled side. This proves to be a turning point in her treatment. Anja doesn't need help regulating her emotions—the woman is a regulation machine. The moment she feels a twinge of distress, she engages in some type of doctor-approved coping skill that ultimately prevents her from experiencing her internal world.

While leaning into our pain and discomfort can certainly be unpleasant, it is essential for experiencing the full spectrum of our emotions. As author Brené Brown puts it, "If we numb the dark, we numb the light," (Brown, 2018). In effect, Anja has created a cycle in which she is numb to most of her internal experiences.

Thus, instead of giving her new interventions to try, I suggest that she do *less*.

For overcontrolled individuals like Anja, this is not an easy ask. Not only can it be challenging for them to break the habit of immediately moving to a coping skill when discomfort arises, but it's even more challenging to sit with a painful experience, thought, or emotion without doing anything to relieve the pressure. These individuals often worry that allowing themselves to settle into their feelings, rather than working to reduce them, will cause them to lose control, manifesting in undesirable behaviors such as crying, yelling, or lashing out at others. The way Anja hears it at first, I'm suggesting that she go against her mental muscle memory, against her parents' teachings, against the socially accepted "fact" that copious self-control can only be a good thing. Instead of offering her another intervention to do when she was upset, I tell her that we need to work on helping her activate her social safety systems and simply be curious about what she is experiencing without doing anything to change her internal state. Essentially, the woman needs to chill out. This isn't as cavalier as it sounds—research tells us that the most beneficial interventions for overcontrolled coping are those that "prioritize the value of seeking pleasure, relaxing control, and joining with others" (Lynch, 2018). In other words, no goals to achieve, no milestones to conquer, no objective except to, well, chill.

The "no objective" part is perhaps the most important. The moment the activity becomes goal-oriented, it's no longer flexible, pleasure-focused, or socially connecting; instead it becomes a performance-based task with a specific end goal and a "right" way of doing it. For instance, Anja loves doing puzzles, but as soon as the puzzle presents a challenge, pleasure and connection go out the window, and Anja attacks that puzzle like it's the final mile in a World Marathon Major.

Despite Anja's initial chagrin, we get creative in finding ways for her to engage in activities that can't be framed in the context of goals or achievement. The following are some ideas we come up with:

- Watching clouds (Yep, you read that right. And no, you are not allowed to turn it into a competition.)
- Abstract art activities (Abstract because there is no "right" way of doing this.)
- Listening to music
- Moving her body (e.g., dance, stretch, do anything without any guidelines)

Another treatment method for supporting folks with overcontrolled coping is the exercise of self-inquiry. An essential intervention within the RO-DBT model, this exercise has individuals pause and conduct an internal examination of themselves anytime they notice discomfort arising. Instead of moving toward one of their go-to regulating skills or even a healthy distraction, they purposefully orient themselves toward their distress in order to learn from it. It can be helpful for them to have a journal and a couple of go-to questions to ask themselves, specifically questions that move them away from problem-solving, justifying, or blaming, and instead toward curiosity and acceptance.

This exercise differs from a typical coping skill in that the purpose is not regulation or even feeling better, at least in the moment. While thoughtfully and intentionally engaging with yourself can certainly lessen your distress, the goal here is to steer into the skid, as it were, instead of jerking the wheel to avoid any possible pain.

Wondering what you're supposed to ask yourself in this self-inquiry process? (If you lean toward overcontrolled coping, you're probably also wondering, "How many questions do I need?" and "Which ones are most effective?" and "Do you have a list of them somewhere I can reference?") While I don't mean to be intentionally vague, part of the intent of this exercise is to be more experimental and less structured. With that in mind, I'll just give you one question to get your self-inquiry started. Ask yourself, "What can I learn from this?" and then allow yourself the freedom to pursue any other questions that naturally follow.

Undercontrolled Coping Style

Now that you've met Anja, let me introduce you to her wife Tami.

Tami is one of those people whose vibrancy is contagious. Where Anja's emotional expressiveness is on the lower end, Tami wears her heart proudly on her sleeve, getting excited about even the smallest things. People enjoy being around Tami because she makes everything more fun and lively, and she seems to feel their emotions as deeply as her own.

Still, while Tami and those around her enjoy her heightened responses to everyday life, she sometimes feels like her emotions control her. Along with having trouble regulating her emotions, she can be impulsive and struggle with controlling her behavior at times. Individuals like Tami may also suffer from mental health conditions such as depression, anxiety, borderline personality disorder, substance use disorders, or binge eating disorders. Tami often thinks that having more self-control would help her feel less exhausted from trying to resist each urge she experiences.

We will explore strategies that can help Tami manage and tolerate these feelings. But before we get to the how, let's spend some more time on the why.

Here Come the Firefighters

Think back to our old friend the manager from Chapter 1, that protective part of ourselves that can result in behaviors such as perfectionism, people-pleasing, and impression management. Well, it's time to meet one of our other protective parts, which IFS has termed our "firefighters."

If the firefighters had a motto, it would be "Whatever it takes." While managers worry about the way we are perceived and how others think of us, the firefighters have no such qualms. True to their name, firefighters invade the burning house that is your dysregulated system with a singular mission: damage control. They don't give a crap about how clean your home is or what your neighbor might think. All they care about is helping you put out that fire by whatever means necessary.

The firefighter part of you developed to protect the more vulnerable parts of yourself, the parts that you fear others will judge, dislike, or misunderstand. Our firefighters will do whatever it takes to keep these parts safe and your distress low, even if it means engaging in numbing behaviors like mindlessly scrolling your phone for hours or drinking until you don't remember what you were upset about.

Nevertheless, I stand by my earlier assertion that you have no bad parts. Your firefighters' motives are benevolent, and while their intervention can have unhealthy and even dangerous outcomes at times, they can also guide us into certain behaviors that are helpful. For example, take our discussion of self-soothing in Chapter 2. This essential coping skill is brought in by our firefighters to help us regulate our emotions and manage our distress. While I know way too much about the multi-million-dollar real estate business, thanks to that self-soothing Netflix binge, my distress has been reduced to a tolerable level as a result. And while I don't love that I spent most of my time at that party scrolling through my phone in a dark corner, it was the mindless break I needed before reengaging with the crowd.

So how does all this relate to self-control? How can people like Tami manage their wild and wonderful feelings without going into full "robot" mode?

When my clients tell me that they struggle with self-control and continue to engage in behaviors that go against their values, they often confess a feeling of shame or a sense that they must be lazy or undisciplined. My first response is to remind them that the fact that they are in therapy tells me they are anything but lazy, and the same goes for you reading this book. Second, I encourage them (and you) to pay attention to the "uncontrolled" part of you. The part that goes off on your partner. The part that prompts you to eat more than you would like, drink more than you intended to, or do anything that goes against the kind of person you aspire to be. That part of you isn't activated at random—it does what it does with a purpose. In other words, there is a reason your firefighter parts urges you to engage in these specific behaviors. Before these behaviors can change, we need to explore the triggers that call your firefighters to the scene.

It's worth noting that your firefighters may come on extra strong at times because they're protecting a part of you that has endured significant trauma. If this is the case, engaging in psychotherapy with an IFS therapist could be incredibly beneficial (in my completely unbiased opinion). Regardless, the end goal is not to rid yourself of your firefighter parts, but rather to change your relationship with them. If your firefighter parts recognize that you are paying attention to them and are taking measures to keep yourself safe, they will feel less need to unleash a full arsenal of "protective" impulses.

Exercise

MEET AND GREET WITH YOUR FIREFIGHTERS

If you haven't already, take a minute to think about your own firefighters and the behaviors that bring relief in the short-term, but leave you feeling frustrated, disappointed, regretful. In the space provided, draw a picture of these parts of you. There are no guidelines for what this picture needs to include and how big or how small it may be.

Now that you have your firefighters visualized, ask them the following questions and journal your responses.

- What is your hope for me?
- How are you trying to help me?

- When did you first start coming around?
- What would you be doing if it wasn't this?
- Anything else you want to tell me?

Thank these parts for sharing whatever they did, and write your reflections below.

Urge Surfing

As with many exercises in this book, engaging with your firefighter parts will be a long-term work-in-progress. And just like any other relationship you have, there will be easier times when you and your firefighters act in serene symbiosis, as well as times when things get so stressful that your firefighters come barreling onto the scene, lights flashing and siren screaming.

For those stressful moments, let me introduce you to "urge surfing." Unfortunately, it's not as fun as the name implies. Originally derived from DBT, urge surfing is aimed at helping individuals tolerate their urges without responding to them. This intervention has been used for a variety of serious issues and conditions, including binge eating disorders and substance use disorders, but it can also be just as useful for "milder" concerns like emotional eating, texting your ex (again), or even apologizing when you know there is no reason for you to do so.

As a rule, an impulse or urge can last up to twenty minutes before it hits peak intensity; then like the cresting of a wave, it gradually subsides. This exercise is designed to help you overcome the urge, not by ignoring it, but by confronting it head-on and riding out its intensity until it peaks, crashes, and disappears. The more you practice, the less your urges will control your behavior—instead, you'll be the one in control.

Below I've provided a script to help you learn to "surf." Choose the urge that you find most problematic lately, and let's get in those waves together.

Exercise

URGE SURFING

Find a comfortable location with minimal distractions, and allow your mind to settle on the urge you've chosen. Imagine this urge in front of you taking the shape of a wave. The more intense the urge becomes, the bigger the wave grows. You are not the wave, nor are you swimming in it; you are the surfer on top of the wave, riding it out. At times it feels like the wave's momentum will never end. Eventually the wave builds to a gigantic peak, then—as it always will—it falls and gradually flattens out. Allow yourself to stay in this comfortable position as you observe the rising and falling of the waves until you eventually find yourself back on the shore.

How was that for you? I haven't been surfing because I'm terrified of being eaten by sharks, but from what I hear, surfing for the first time means falling off the board—not once, but a lot. By the end, you are bone-tired and maybe even feeling a little hopeless—will you ever be like one of those badass surfers in *Blue Crush* whose prowess on their boards is outshone only by their perfectly tousled beach hair?

Hair aside, it takes a lot of practice to get to a *Blue Crush* level of surfing . . . and that is just as true for this type of psychological surfing, as well. You'll need quite a bit of practice before you feel fully comfortable confronting the waves of your urges. The rougher the conditions are, the more challenging the ride becomes—make sure to get plenty of practice with this new skill when your urges are at low tide, so that when storms bring the big swells in, you'll be ready.

Happy surfing . . . and look out for sharks!

Self-Talk

Merriam-Webster Dictionary: *Talk or thoughts directed at oneself.*

Urban Dictionary: *Self-talk is the way you talk to yourself, or your inner voice. You might not be aware that you're doing it, but you almost certainly are.*

Self-talk is important because it has a big impact on how you feel and what you do.

APA Dictionary of Psychology: *An internal dialogue in which an individual utters phrases or sentences to himself or herself. Negative self-talk often confirms and reinforces negative beliefs and attitudes, such as fears and false aspirations, which have a correspondingly negative effect on the individual's feelings (e.g., a sense of worthlessness) and reactions (e.g., demotivation). In certain types of psychotherapy, one of the tasks of the therapist is to encourage the client to replace self-defeating, negative self-talk with more constructive, positive self-talk. In sport, athletes are trained to use positive self-talk to cue the body to act in particular ways, to cue attentional focus, to motivate, to reinforce self-efficacy, and to facilitate the creation of an ideal performance state.*

5

SELF-TALK

You know, there are some real gems about self-talk on social media. For example, take this brief but impactful post from IG: "Check your self-talk twice as often as you check your phone."

Damn—gold! I love the idea of redirecting our doom-scrolling energy toward our internal dialogue.

Here's another one I like: "Notice your extreme thoughts by noticing your use of words such as never, always, all, or nothing."

So good. (And I'm not just saying that because it was written by a psychologist.)

Unfortunately, posts on authentic or automatic self-talk were in the minority. Want to guess what the majority of #selftalk social posts focus on? That's right—it's all about the positive affirmations, y'all. Most of social media's advice on self-talk is focused on speaking positively to yourself and doing everything you can to drive out negativity. I'm talking pithy quotes such as, "Don't be a victim to negative self-talk, practice positive self-talk always," and profound graphics showing how "I'm a bad person" can be transformed into "I make mistakes and am learning to do better."

The general theme of these posts is not inherently problematic. However, setting the expectation that healthy self-talk should be exclusively empowering, confident, and have a consistent "everything is awesome" vibe can actually leave readers feeling disempowered and confused when they're not able to switch their negative self-talk into positive self-talk as easily as these posts portray.

In reality our self-talk is based on our history, the conditions of our current environment, and the seemingly random thoughts, images, words, and sensations that appear in our consciousness throughout the day. In other words, self-talk is not as controllable as these posts make it out to be. Rather, many of our immediate thoughts that influence our self-talk are echoes of our history rather than intentional, selected ideas that reflect our current values. For example, when I start to notice myself feeling emotional around my friends, my immediate reaction is often, *OMG, shut it down. Don't lose it right now and embarrass yourself.*

To be clear, this is the self-talk that arises in the moment, but it is certainly not talk or messaging that I agree with. Rather, it reflects lessons and experiences I have internalized from childhood, past relationships, and society's messaging toward women that influence this in-the-moment self-talk. I was not able to control those immediate thoughts from filtering in, what I do have power over is choosing what thoughts I want to invest in.

If we can allow ourselves to simply notice and name the thought, without fighting it or attempting to shut it down, we give ourselves the opportunity to consciously create self-talk that feels helpful and congruent with our values. Before we go there though, let's explore how we get stuck fighting our internal experiences.

The Toxic Culture of Positive Affirmations

I have a visceral reaction when a client proclaims that they want to work on "positive thinking" or recite more affirmations to themselves. My eye actually twitches as every part of me protests against the intense pressure clients put on themselves to float through the world without one stray negative thought entering their minds.

To be clear, I'm not some ogre who denounces all efforts to be positive. For the longest time, I kept a written affirmation in my purse that said, "I am learning to accept myself as I am." I felt so reassured every time I read it. In fact, I'm so pro-affirmation that I feel bad for the amount of pressure we put on these affirmations to drive away our negative thoughts, increase our confidence, and solve all that ails us.

Take, for example, my client Nina, who has decided to finally confront her mother about how she passive-aggressively criticizes Nina's relationship, sometimes even in front of Nina and her partner. (With, I might add, a particular focus on how much she misses Nina's ex—awkward!) In the past, Nina has tried redirecting the conversation or offering subtle hints about how this makes her feel, yet her mom continues to make these comments. As Nina works up the courage to speak to her mom about this painful topic, she is collecting positive affirmations like they are ninja stars she can throw to deflect any of her mom's potential responses. Here's how that plan worked out for her:

MOM: I just think Ravi was so pleasant. I think we can agree he was more your level, if you know what I mean.

NINA (internally): *I am at peace with who I am and with my relationship. But my god, if she says one more think about Ravi . . . okay, just remember: I am peaceful, I am enough. We are channeling the peace.*

MOM: I mean, I think this is just that sensitivity problem you have. You know how you get.

NINA (internally): *I am at peace with who I am, and I am enough. Wow, right back to criticizing me again. This is fun, this is familiar . . . okay, hold on, something about peace. Yes, peace. But seriously, calling me sensitive again?! I have told her how much that word hurts hundreds of . . . nope, nope, you are not doing this. You are a peaceful being and . . . there was something else . . . oh right—you are enough!*

MOM: Luckily, I've invited Ravi over today so you guys can get reacquainted. Don't worry, I bought something else for you to wear, because I think we both know green is not your color.

NINA (internally): *I am at peace with who I am . . . Oh my god, I am not at peace. My head hurts, I'm pissed, and I'm going to lose it!*

Positive affirmations are not inherently toxic or unbeneficial, but when they are used as a weapon to combat the appearance of negative thoughts, feelings, or experiences, they can become just as dangerous as other maladaptive coping mechanisms, such as drinking, binge eating, or engaging in risky behaviors that allow us to avoid and distract from immediate pain but certainly do not set us up for long-term health or happiness.

Another danger of positive affirmations is when they become divisively gendered. I found a fascinating tidbit in my research that shows how much self-talk (and its underlying the messages) can differ between men and women.

Here are some examples of posts for #selftalkwomen:

- "I radiate positive energy and warmth."
- "I am worthy of love and care."
- "I choose to live in a way that brings joy and love to others and myself."

And here are some posts for #selftalkmen:

- "I will train hard to achieve my target."
- "I will do what it takes to reach my goal."
- "I will make things work for me today."

That first list sounds like someone is training to be a literal angel, while the second list sounds like a candidate for *American Ninja Warrior*. This disparity further reinforces the painful narrative that women need to exist in a state of perpetual serenity for the sake of serving others, while men get to pump themselves up to take action on behalf of their own goals.

Gender stereotypes aside, the mainstream embrace of affirmations has only strengthened the pressure we feel to control and manipulate our self-talk. When we try to control our internal experience this way, even an empowering statement can get us more stuck in negativity, which makes us double down on our efforts to control. There's nothing more disempowering than fighting against the reality of what you're thinking in the moment—it's like trying to climb out of quicksand. As counterintuitive as it may sound, the less you fight against your internal experiences, the more empowered you'll feel regarding your self-talk. To put it another way, the less you pit positive affirmations against your negative thoughts, the more freedom your self-talk has to become whatever you choose.

Positive Self-Talk Versus Negative Self-Talk: The Ultimate Battle

Imagine if the "celebrities" of the mental health scene were put into a WWE fighting ring. I'm talking a lineup of all the most popular therapists and thought leaders—one that would have the Enneagram-loving, breathwork-practicing masses lined up outside like they're waiting for Brené Brown's latest book release. The final matchup in this event would be—*dun dun dun*—the ultimate battle: Positive Self-Talk versus Negative Self-Talk. (*Rahhh!*—the fans go wild!)

This is the epic battle that is always raging on the topic of self-talk. As much as I love a good cage fight, there is way too much absolutism in this way of thinking. I'm definitely in favor enjoying our positive thoughts by focusing on them, repeating them, writing them down, even stitching them on a pillow to annoy our guests. What we don't need to do is force out our negative self-talk anytime it shows up, and we definitely don't need to decide that having it show up at all means something must be fundamentally wrong with us.

What having negative self-talk doesn't mean:

- Something is wrong with you.
- You hate yourself or have incredibly low self-esteem.
- You need to do something immediately to make this negative self-talk stop.
- If you don't do something immediately, your negative self-talk will linger forever and haunt your hopes and dreams.
- You might as well quit working toward all the things you want/you'll never be able to enjoy the things you currently have.

What having negative self-talk means:

- You are breathing, and your brain is functioning.
- Your brain is constantly producing countless thoughts, images, and words each day that encompass the entire emotional spectrum.
- You've heard these statements or messages from others, and something in your environment may have triggered them coming to the forefront.
- You may have protector parts (remember Esmerelda from chapter 1?) that want to look out for you.

Let's pause on that last point for a moment. To refresh your memory, our protector parts often show up in people-pleasing or perfectionistic ways when they are concerned that your needs may not be met. In moments when your negative self-talk is feeling out of control, it likely means that something in your current environment triggered those protector parts to come to the "rescue" with their critical commentary.

In the end, the "flavor" of your self-talk matters a lot less than the meaning you attach to it.

We Can't Turn Off the Radio, But We Can Adjust the Volume

"I just want to be able to control my self-talk."

Whenever I hear that phrase in therapy, my own self-talk responds, *Damn, I'm about to be the bearer of bad news again.*

It makes total sense that we want to ensure that everything our mind "plays" for us is empowering, motivating, and congruent with our hopes, dreams, and values. The positive self-talk crowd seems to think that you can curate your thoughts like you would a Spotify playlist, queuing up only the tunes you want to listen to, with the right intensity, the right pacing, even the right timing for what you need in the moment. (You've got your "Going Out" playlist with those party-ready jams, and your "I'm a Badass" playlist to pump you up before important presentations.) You don't have to listen to songs you are not interested in or commercials that bore you. You are riding a musical wave that takes you exactly where you want to go and keeps you feeling good all the way there.

However, your mind is more like a radio than a Spotify playlist. Sometimes you get a day of songs you mostly like, while other days it's music you hate or have never heard of. Occasionally, you get one of those moments you live for, when your favorite nostalgic summer jam comes on and you turn the volume up, roll the windows down, and scream-sing your way through every note. But then, inevitably, a commercial comes on. Or worse, a rerun of the morning talk show. Or worst of all, as I mentioned earlier, that Bruno Mars song "Marry You." At that point, you might knock the volume back down and look out the window until it passes, or perhaps you start yelling, "Boooo!" and lecturing your passengers on why this garbage should not be allowed on the radio.

Still following my analogy? As much as we want it to be, our mind is not a resource we can control, which means we can't perfectly curate its contents. We may be able to influence what goes through it by choosing where to tune in (i.e., find positive environments and people to be around), but we can't stop the negative messages from showing up. All we can control is how we respond to what we hear and what meaning we ultimately attach to it.

For example, have you ever noticed the more you hate a song, the more you seem to hear it everywhere? And even when it's not coming through a store speaker or a stranger's earbuds, it just keeps playing on a hellish loop in your head? It works the same way with our minds. The more we argue, debate, or negate (*ha!*) our negative self-talk, the more room it takes up in our mind. Since completely ignoring our negative self-talk doesn't work (nobody puts Esmerelda in a corner!), we can learn to be curious about what it wants to tell us.

Let's see what this could have looked like with our girl Nina.

MOM: I just think Ravi was so pleasant. I think we can agree he was more your level, if you know what I mean.

NINA (internally): *I am at peace with who I am and my relationship . . . You know what? I* don't *feel peaceful. I'm upset and feel like I'm being talked down to. I just feel annoyed and disappointed that I'm having this same conversation again.*

MOM: I mean, I think this is just that sensitivity problem you have. You know how you get.

NINA (internally): *I do know how I get. I have all the feelings that I'm having now, and trying to avoid them only makes me go off. Hmmm . . . I would like to do things differently. I think my mom and I both deserve to not repeat the same awful conversations again and again . . . or, at least, try not to.*

MOM: Luckily, I've invited Ravi over today so you guys can get reacquainted. Don't worry, I bought something else for you to wear because I think we both know green is not your color.

NINA: Hey Mom, I get that you are trying to help me, but we've been here before and had this exact same conversation. Would you be open to having a do-over?

Now in a fantasy world, Nina's mom would accept this gracious invitation and restart the conversation, this time attuning herself to Nina's discomfort and even to her own sense of urgency in trying to force the same conversation again. In the real world, Nina's mom may not accept this invitation, because her internal radio is playing a special all-day marathon of "Fix Nina's Life ASAP." But regardless of what her mom does, Nina has succeeded in turning up the volume on the self-talk that matters to her. It might not have been positive in the social media-approved sense, but it did help her act in congruence with her values.

Let's Turn Down the Volume

Turning down the volume of some thoughts is not easy; at times, it's straight up impossible. There may be moments when you are feeling dysregulated to such a degree that the critical-thinking parts of your brain go temporarily offline. When that's the case, adjusting your radio starts with moving yourself into a "window of tolerance"—that is, an optimal state of arousal in which you feel alert but not overwhelmed.

In a situation where you are stressed but not completely overwhelmed, one method for turning down the volume is to practice observing without judgment. Let's do it right now. Take a look around you and tell me five things you see in your surroundings. I'll wait.

Got your five things? Did what you notice include any value judgments? ("I see an old coffee thermos. Man, I need to clean that out. I see a shit ton of wires—why does one device need so many wires?") Try it again, but this time, focus on observing your environment *without* value judgments. ("I see a coffee thermos, a laptop charger, a phone charger, ear buds, and an extension cord.") Notice the difference?

Want to see this technique in action? I'll give you a situation of my own, hot off the press. I just left a meeting in which I shared some sappy feelings of appreciation for how my team always shows up and supports each other. In the moment, it seemed well received, and I mentally patted myself on the back for actually un-muting myself during a meeting and being so eloquent as a result. (Or as my self-talk put it, *Go me!*) Then as often happens, doubt and anxiety start to creep in. As I play back my mental tape of the meeting, my commentary goes something like this:

- *Ugh, that felt weird—I shouldn't have said that.*
- *It didn't seem like people were smiling enough after I made that joke.*
- *Did my tone sound fake? It wasn't fake, but I bet they think I was being fake.*
- *I realize applause would have been weird . . . but I wish there had been applause.*

Welcome to my mind. Now let's see what happens if I take the value judgments away from the observations.

- *I had an emotional reaction after sharing in my meeting.*
- *Several people shared their reaction to what I had to say.*
- *The meeting ended a couple of minutes after I shared.*
- *My tone may change when I share this kind of thing in a meeting compared to other contexts.*

I have to tell y'all, my chest just got a little lighter writing that out. Instead of trying to immediately think positively or ruminate in the negativity of self-doubt, I'm simply observing my internal experience, so that I can consciously decide how I want to talk to myself about it. If the self-talk that results is positive, it will be all the more effective for being authentic.

If we follow the narrative of the positive affirmation pushers, we reinforce rigidity, all-or-nothing thinking, and conditional self-love. Rather than forcing any tonality on our self-talk, we can choose to become observers of our internal dialogue—notice it, wonder about it, and then decide how to act based on this thoughtful reflection. Self-talk is much more powerful when we choose our own narrative.

Self-ish

Merriam-Webster Dictionary: *Concerned excessively or exclusively with oneself: seeking or concentrating on one's own advantage, pleasure, or well-being without regard for others.*

Urban Dictionary: *When you have a huge amount of interest invested in yourself, or when you don't think about the wants and needs of others.*

APA Dictionary of Psychology: *The tendency to act excessively or solely in a manner that benefits oneself, even if others are disadvantaged.*

6

SELF-ISH

Were you starting to wonder if this book was ever going to actually talk about selfishness? Well, spoiler alert, we've actually been exploring selfishness all along—just not the simplified version many of us have been taught. Let's get to the real, multi-layered definition of selfish and learn how allowing a little bit of selfishness in your life may be one of the best things you can do for your mental health.

If the title of this book tells you anything, you can guess that I am pro-selfishness. Now, this doesn't mean I'm pro "not giving a fuck about anyone else." I made a career out of supporting and caring for people precisely because I give lots of fucks! When I say I'm pro-selfishness, I mean that I am pro "giving yourself the space, time, and attention you deserve." I am pro "allowing yourself the same respect, dignity, and compassion you give to others." I am pro "taking lots of time, energy, and whatever else you need to make your life what you want it to be." Essentially I am pro-you.

Even if you agree with me, you might still struggle with the fear of being perceived as selfish. If so, I understand this completely and certainly grappled with trying to internalize this concept myself. In fact, I went through this dreadful phase of asking clients how the word "self-ful" sat with them as an alternative to "selfish." I gag when I look back on this—did I really feel so much discomfort with crossing a social taboo that I had to invent a new word? Apologies, past clients, for not modeling that it is completely okay, appropriate, and beneficial to your psychological well-being to prioritize your own needs.

We don't need to dilute concepts to make them more palatable. By turning selfish into self-ful, we're only reinforcing the stigma against being concerned with ourselves, our well-being, and our needs. Speaking of stigma, when I consult the next set of "experts"—our old friends, the social media platforms—many of the #selfish posts focus on the supposed link between selfishness and narcissism. ("Narcissist" is another psychological term that has been heavily misunderstood in social media and society generally, but I'll leave that soapbox for another time.) On the other hand, I also see many posts that appear to be in favor of selfishness, such as:

- "Be selfish" (Simple. Direct. I like it.)
- "Sometimes you gotta be selfish" (Sensing a theme here.)
- "I'm definitely in a selfish phase in my life right now. It's all about ME . . . ME . . . ME." (I hope this phase continues, and you'll see why soon.)
- "You're not selfish for wanting to be treated well." (Though maybe you are, and that's okay too.)

With so many contrasting and divisive ideas out there, how do we allow selfishness into our lives in a way that is congruent with the kind of person we strive to be? To answer these questions, it's time to explore this concept in action.

The Selfish Woman

Let's start with consulting the *Merriam-Webster* definition, an interesting two-part definition that starts off explaining selfish as being "generally concerned with oneself." So far, so good. It's the second part that makes us pause. Read it again: "without regard for others." I believe this sums up the fundamental challenge we face when considering the concept of selfishness. We become so concerned about being perceived as not caring for others that we overcorrect to the point of not having any concern for ourselves.

While being called selfish has a negative connotation for anyone, there is even more stigma in being called a selfish woman. As women, we are conditioned by societal norms, family traditions, and internalized pressures to be giving, nurturing, caring, and compassionate, to the point that these words are considered practically synonymous with *feminine* and *womanly*. In contrast, selfish is their antithesis, the ultimate insult against womanhood.

This dilemma may even find itself in the most personal of our decisions: the ones about our fertility. I'll illustrate this by sharing a time when I was called "selfish" for a choice I made. After my daughter was born, my husband and I discussed the possibility of having a second child.

Through talking at length about what it meant to us to have children and how we visualized the concept of family, we decided we only wanted to have one child. A lot of reasoning went into this decision, but I'll admit some of the reasons had to do with our desire to prioritize ourselves. We both have careers we are passionate about, as well as side hustles and hobbies we love. We are pretty passionate about our relationship too. While we worried about the potential impact on our daughter of not having siblings (particularly since we both came from big families), we ultimately saw that this choice would preserve our capacity to be the present, loving, attuned parents we wanted to be. As a bonus, we could all fit on one airplane aisle with three seats instead of having to divide up and sit next to randos. Score!

While we had many amazing folks in our lives who supported our choice (it helps that the majority of my friends are therapists), we did have a few people who called our choice—you guessed it—selfish. Some even proclaimed that our daughter would be selfish because she did not have any siblings, who would presumably serve as the morality police for her.

My response to those comments? "Good! I'm glad you see that Michael and I are prioritizing ourselves so that we can be the best versions of ourselves. And hell yes, I hope my daughter is selfish and recognizes that her needs matter."

My decision to carry another child in my body was uniquely my own, and the decision to have no more children was a decision I shared only with my husband—after all, no one else would be raising this child for us. Yet as the continuing battle for women's reproductive autonomy has shown all too well, a woman's fertility choices can be described as selfish no matter what they are. Have only one kid? Selfish—who will play with that child when y'all go on vacation? Have a bunch of kids? Selfish—have you seen the environment lately? Have no kids? Selfish—what about your parents' dreams of being grandparents?

I'm not arguing that we shouldn't strive for these important qualities of compassion, caring, and nurturance—in fact, I think we *all* should, no matter who we are and what gender, if any, we identify with. Instead, I'm arguing that while there may be times when we prioritize the needs of others over ourselves, there are also times when we are allowed to put our needs at the top. For example, while I made the "selfish" decision to only have one child, I have prioritized my child's needs over my own in nearly every decision that has followed. For example, Michael and I are fortunate to have childcare options that allow us to either be working or doing our own things Monday through Friday from 8:00 to 5:00. However, I have created a work schedule that ends on Tuesdays and Thursdays at 1:00 p.m. so that my daughter and I can have outings and adventures, like going to the playground or the children's museum, or just random fun activities in the house like putting dry noodles on straws (harder than it sounds). Sure, I could spend that time working and bringing in more income, or I could spend it on me time (working out, leisure, napping), but I choose to prioritize one-on-one time with my daughter because of how important she is to me.

Similarly, there are the countless little actions that all parents do to prioritize our children's needs that often go unnoticed, such as getting their dinner on the plate first even when you are starving, waiting patiently by the toilet for them to pee while doing a little jig to distract yourself from your own need to use the bathroom, and of course, let's not forget sleep, from middle-of-the-night wake-ups to early morning rises. (Does 4:00 a.m. count as an early morning rise or does it just all run together at that point?) We do this because we love our children and are committed to their care, happiness, and health. However, in order to be this attentive and attuned to their needs, we need to care for ourselves. From time to time, this means prioritizing our needs over everyone else's. (We'll talk more about being a selfish parent in Chapter 10.)

Making Selfish Moves

So, have you started thinking yet about how you could be a little more selfish?

When I ask clients this question, I can often see the overwhelm arise as they search for any area of their life where they feel comfortable focusing on their own needs over those of their family and friends: *I mean, if I am more selfish in this area, it's going to affect my partner, which will affect their job, which will affect our livelihood, which means we will have to move back in with my parents, and then he'll hate me forever.* Damn, that got dark quickly.

Maybe that's how you're feeling now . . . or maybe your mind did one of its greatest tricks: it became a "yes, but" machine.

Yes, it would be helpful to change my work hours by thirty minutes so I could have that extra time in the morning to myself, but *work is really busy right now, so maybe I can wait till the next quarter.*

Yes, I would love it if my parents didn't bring their dogs to our house because they always pee on the furniture, but *my mom is so sensitive, and they did drive all the way across town to see us.*

Yes, I did ask my husband to wake up with our daughter this morning and take care of her so I could focus on writing this chapter, but *it's definitely past her breakfast time, which means they are probably still upstairs watching baby TV on his phone . . . so I'll just get her breakfast myself.*

What do we do when we notice the "yes, but" machine taking over? We do our trick from Chapter 3—name it to tame it! The more aware you become of how this pattern shows up in your life, the more you're able to decide how much attention to pay to it. In my experience, it never pays to fight the "yes, buts." Don't debate or bargain with them, and definitely don't try to convince them why your "selfish" course of action makes sense. Just allow yourself to notice and name them, acknowledge your reaction to them, and then keep on keeping on.

If you've managed to ignore the "yes, buts," but still find yourself stuck imagining what selfish move you could make, try identifying a woman in your life that you care deeply about and, in your opinion, could stand to be a little more selfish. Once you've got someone in mind, imagine one tiny yet specific "dose" of selfishness that would benefit this woman's life.

I think immediately of my younger sister, who will inconvenience herself to an incredible degree if it means avoiding hurting someone's feelings or ensuring everyone else's needs get met. Case in point: for over a decade now, she has gone with my mother to get their eyebrows threaded at a store that is minutes from the house we grew up in, but at least forty minutes from where my sister lives now (not to mention the scheduling gymnastics required to coordinate their schedules with their preferred eyebrow threader). Nevertheless, she still makes this trip without fail twice a month! Is it a sweet, shared ritual that helps them connect? Yes! Is it a massive time suck and a consistent source of annoyance for my sister? Also yes.

With that example in mind, try choosing at least three women in your life and identify at least one selfish move they could make that would make their lives a little easier and would allow them to focus on their own needs a little more. I'll get you started with my example.

Exercise

Woman: *(Example)* My sister Sheila

Selfish move: Find an eyebrow threader closer to her house, and schedule a solo appointment with them. Inform Mom she will no longer be doing eyebrow appointments with her but will still see her every week at family dinner.

Woman 1: ______________________________

Selfish move: ______________________________

____

____

____

____

____

Woman 2: ______________________________

Selfish move: ______________________________

____

____

____

____

____

Woman 3: ______________________________

Selfish move: ______________________________

____

____

____

____

____

I'm guessing you can see where this is going. Now that you are in brainstorming mode, take a moment to consider three selfish moves you could make in your own life. Remember, your moves can be as small as taking an extra five minutes in the morning to make the delicious coffee with the frothed milk instead of the K-cup, or as big as finally quitting that bowling league you dread every week but feel guilty for leaving. Just as much as the women in your life matter and will benefit from some selfish moves, so will you!

Exercise

My selfish move: ______________________________

____

____

____

____

____

____

My selfish move: ____________________

____

____

____

____

____

____

My selfish move: ____________________

____

____

____

____

____

Imagine a world in which these women, including yourself, made the brilliant moves you have identified for them. Imagine a generation of children who grew up understanding that it is normal, healthy, and acceptable to focus on their own needs. Imagine the new sense of ease in our social situations and relationships that would come from our collective understanding that we can prioritize and communicate about what we need. Imagine how our lives would change if, instead of using our precious energy to suppress our desires (and the resulting resentment), we redirected that energy into our passions, our hobbies, and yes, our relationships!

Finding a way to ensure others are cared for even as we focus on caring for ourselves—isn't that just like a woman? As counterintuitive as it may seem, prioritizing your own needs can help you pull off that multitasking magic women are famous for. Try adding a dose of selfishness to your life, and find out for yourself. (With any luck, it will be contagious to those amazing women on your list.)

Is the Self-Help Movement Selfish?

I recently came across a podcast that posed the question above. My immediate response was defensive: "Of course it isn't! The self-help movement is adaptive, healthy, and psychologically appropriate." And this was while writing a book advocating for selfishness!

My reaction shows how ingrained our resistance is to being called selfish. After thinking about it some more, I've changed my stance to a yes—I do think the self-help movement is selfish, and rightfully so. The purpose of this movement is to encourage us to dedicate time, resources, and ourselves to foster our own well-being, sometimes even prioritizing it over the needs of others. By making these types of selfish choices, we are able to act in ways that are congruent with our values, helping us get closer to being the person we want to be and contribute to the people, causes, and movements that matter to us without burning out in the process.

Furthermore, being selfish does not mean acting in isolation. Sometimes being selfish requires us to ask others for help, whether it's finding a compromise between two competing needs or showing up for us in a way that prioritizes our needs over theirs. (Hard to imagine, right?) When I asked my husband to wake up with our daughter this morning, I was asking him to prioritize my desire to write early in the morning when my mind is the sharpest over his desire to sleep in for another hour.

I recognize that having a partner I can ask for support is a privileged position, and that help is not always accessible to everyone. Still, I encourage you to work together with the people in your life to help each other make some selfish moves. If women being a little more selfish could make the world a more magical place, just imagine the magic that could come from mothers, sisters, and best friends coming together to support each other's selfishness.

The Art of Being Selfish

One of my favorite self-help books is Mark Manson's *The Subtle Art of Not Giving a Fuck*. While the book offers many profound ideas about life and human psychology, Manson acknowledges that folks may assume from the title that it is a treatise on how to stop caring about anything in your life. Your work? No fucks. Other people's problems? No fucks. The world at large? No fucks.

Just like with the concept of selfishness, folks tend to miss the important part of this title—namely, the "subtle" part. Instead of advocating for total disregard of all responsibilities and relationships, Manson advocates that we identify what is *most* important to us and give those things the energy and attention they deserve, while paying way less attention to the things that we don't really give a fuck about.

I often reference this book with my clients when they get stuck ruminating about the sources of stress in their lives. It doesn't always land the first time—I remember one client, after we had discussed this concept, proclaimed that she didn't give any fucks about her job.

"Untrue," I gently responded. "You clearly give many fucks, or it wouldn't have been the dominant topic of our sessions for the past year."

That seemed to snap something in place for her. She realized that, while she truly didn't find any value or meaning in many aspects of her work, she found herself frequently ruminating on those very aspects, both in and outside of therapy. She didn't want to spend so much energy on something she cared so little about, yet she didn't know how to disrupt this cycle.

This is where the subtle artistry comes in: identifying where we want to intentionally direct more energy and care and learning to give less energy and care to everything else. For this client, more energy went toward the quality of her work and mentoring younger female professionals, while less energy went into managing her boss's mercurial moods or ensuring that everyone liked her all the time.

We cannot be selfish in each and every choice we make. Instead, just as my client did, we need to consider when, how, and for what purpose we want to be selfish, and consider the same questions about being self*less*. Each of us must choose for ourselves what really matters and when it's appropriate to override our needs—after all, we are the only ones who know our needs well enough to make that choice.

Self-Esteem

Merriam-Webster Dictionary: *A confidence and satisfaction in oneself.*

Urban Dictionary: *Refers to the way in which people view themselves and their worth. Low self-esteem is a common symptom of depression. Signs include shyness, anxiety about appearance or competence, feelings of worthlessness, and unnecessary guilt or shame.*

What every girl on Girls Gone Wild lacks.

APA Dictionary of Psychology: *The degree to which the qualities and characteristics contained in one's self-concept are perceived to be positive. It reflects a person's physical self-image, view of his or her accomplishments and capabilities, and values and perceived success in living up to them, as well as the ways in which others view and respond to that person. The more positive the cumulative perception of these qualities and characteristics, the higher one's self-esteem. A reasonably high degree of self-esteem is considered an important ingredient of mental health, whereas low self-esteem and feelings of worthlessness are common depressive symptoms.*

7

SELF-ESTEEM

I kept trying to find ways to avoid this chapter. I even thought about replacing it. Whenever I find myself leaning into avoidance, I use the same, *What can I learn from this? What is this discomfort telling me?* exercise we explored in Chapter 4, and what I realized is that—drumroll, please—I had a fear of being exposed as a psychologist who doesn't really understand what self-esteem means. That's almost as bad as being exposed as a psychologist who prefers going to the dentist's office than enduring a thirty-minute meditation. (At least at the dentist's office, you can meditate while sitting in the waiting room. Two birds, one stone, ya know?)

I feel like I should have the answer. It's such a basic concept these days that we begin learning about it in childhood—we may have heard grown-ups use low self-esteem to explain a child's acting out or, on the flip side, grumble about participation trophies as an empty means of boosting self-esteem. A great number my clients come to therapy with the specific goal of developing "good" self-esteem. (Much like saying, "I'm stressed," or "I have anxiety," complaining about self-esteem has become a generic term people use when they are generally unsatisfied with themselves.) But what does this concept really mean?

Once again, social media platforms come through to validate my lack of clarity. The top-performing posts tagged with #selfesteem are mostly helpful, positive, and empowering, but almost none of them directly speak to what self-esteem means. Here are just a few of the #selfesteem posts I found—take a gander for yourself:

- "Narcissists are great at giving you just enough hope to hang onto absolutely nothing."
- "Empathy without boundaries can be self-destructive."
- "Tomorrow is another day full of opportunities."
- "By being yourself, you put something wonderful into the world that wasn't there before."

It seems the internet has not quite agreed on the definition of self-esteem. (Shocking, right?) We know it's important, and that it means something about looking inward and/or doing generally positive things for ourselves, but it seems to be more of a tagalong to the other self-categories we've explored thus far, rather than being its own distinct category. It's as if self-esteem is the random cousin that self-love brought along to the party—sure, she's fine and made herself helpful, but we don't really know why she's here or what to do with her.

Defining Self-Esteem

Each of the definitions of self-esteem tells a slightly different story. *Merriam-Webster*'s definition—our sense of "confidence and satisfaction *in* ourselves"—invites a comparison between self-esteem and self-confidence. It seems that while self-esteem has more to do with our impression of ourselves, self-confidence is more about our trust in our ability to do certain tasks. I may have high self-confidence as a speaker because I know I can present a topic well and keep an audience engaged, but still have low self-esteem regarding who I am as a person. In other words, while self-confidence is easier to exhibit externally, self-esteem is a much more internal experience. (Though that hasn't stopped folks from commenting on each other's perceived self-esteem.)

Next we have good old *Urban Dictionary*, which starts off strong describing self-esteem as how we generally like ourselves, but then reveals its sketchy side by explaining it as "What every girl on *Girls Gone Wild* lacks." I included this offensive, gender-biased part of the definition because it's precisely these kinds of perceptions that distort our understanding of self-esteem.

Finally, we arrive at the ever-reliable American Psychological Association, who lays out a comprehensive definition that characterizes self-esteem as a cumulative assessment of the many parts that make us who we are. This one reminds me of the Cognitive Assessment classes I took in graduate school. I remember that, around that same time, I had an argument with my brother about who was smarter than the other. (Yes, I agree that it's ridiculous that we were having this argument when I was in graduate school.) I was trying to make the point that it wasn't a fair point to say either of us were categorically smarter—instead I said it was more helpful to break down the idea of smartness into its domains such as verbal fluency, nonverbal fluency, and matrix reasoning, then create a cumulative rating based on our totals in these different domains. He called me an idiot, and that was the end of that argument.

Just for fun, let's give self-esteem the same breakdown treatment. For example, your self-assessment may be very positive regarding your capacity to be a supportive friend and loving partner, but perhaps your self-assessment is negative when it comes to how you handle high-pressure situations. Additionally, your self-assessment can be impacted in lasting ways by specific experiences. If you make a joke during a team meeting and everyone dies laughing and says you are just one of the most hilarious people they have ever met, that single moment can make your self-esteem soar long after the joke has been forgotten.

Maybe I'm biased, but I favor the APA's definition. Still while "cumulative assessment" might sound like a scientific way to evaluate self-esteem, it still comes down to the individual—each of our total assessments will be based on our unique understanding of what parts of ourselves we see as having the most value. For example, someone who doesn't prioritize being a supportive friend or loving partner won't feel a hit to their self-esteem if they forget a birthday or anniversary.

With that in mind, the first step in evaluating your own self-esteem process is to consider the parts of yourself that you like or dislike. Which parts of who you are make you the happiest? Which parts do you find yourself ruminating on or wishing you could change? This list is not meant to capture every single aspect of you possible; instead, focus on the parts you care enough to notice or have strong reactions to.

Here's what I came up with:

- My sense of humor
- My capacity to be a loving partner, mother, daughter, and friend
- My ability as a psychologist
- My ability as a leader in my practice
- My physical self-image (specifically my hair being an acceptable level of frizzy and maintaining some level of youthfulness as I trek across my thirties)
- My likability (or my perception of it)
- My capacity to handle things in the moment (e.g., questions during presentations, high-stress situations, etc.)

What ended up on your list? Were there personality traits that you care deeply about? Parts of your body that heavily influence your view of self? Certain abilities that you rely heavily on for work, personal passions, or social situations? (My deep desire to be good at ping pong factors significantly into my self-esteem.) Consider this a living, breathing document that will change and evolve as you grow, just like all the other aspects of the self-relationship that we are exploring—you get to decide what parts matter to you most. And you have the power to define, understand, and rewrite what your self-esteem means to you.

Why Understanding Self-Esteem Matters

Unpacking our self-esteem through this part-by-part assessment allows us to deepen our insight into our values and the parts of ourselves we care to strengthen. There will inevitably be parts of ourselves we struggle to like, feel confident in, or value. For example, I put "my capacity to handle things in the moment" on my self-esteem list precisely because I don't feel great about my ability to handle crises or spontaneity. I remember one time when I started choking on a mint, and my husband immediately started doing the Heimlich maneuver, no questions asked. Had the situation been reversed, I would have asked a million questions, googled the Heimlich maneuver, and probably run around in a circle before taking any real action. All that to say, this is an area where my subjective self-assessment is lower.

This is important because it plays into my overall view of myself. It may be true that I'm an under-functioner in moments of stress; but describing myself this way increases the likelihood that I will fall prey to confirmation bias—that is, I will only pay attention to information that confirms this belief in my inability to save choking people. The move here is not to immediately start countering this view of myself (y'all know by now how I feel about positive affirmations), but rather to pay attention when this view of myself is challenged . . . or, better yet, when I have opportunities to challenge it. For instance, I could take an improv class to help me think better on my feet and expose me to my greatest fear all in one go.

Taking the time to examine your self-esteem can allow you to better understand other challenges or concerns you may be facing. For example, I worked with a client who shared that she had a strong desire to pursue a romantic relationship but was overwhelmed with feelings of discomfort and tension whenever she met someone she liked. She was convinced that low self-esteem was to blame—why else would she be so uncomfortable with an experience she had craved for so long? As we explored her understanding of self-esteem and all the parts that made up her unique view, we also learned more about her history: that she had received little to no consistent loving care growing up, and when she did experience moments of connection, it had often been followed by loss or abandonment. The discomfort she experienced in pursuing a relationship today was very likely triggering fears of going through the same loss of connection she experienced as a child.

We do ourselves a disservice when we chalk up the complexities of our relationships, experiences, and thoughts as wholly determined by our self-esteem without taking the time to uncover what else could be at play. And we definitely do others an injustice when we attempt to categorize them for an experience that is entirely internal. Instead of "rating" your self-esteem as good, bad, poor, or low, let's take the time to truly understand what your self-esteem means to you.

The Generational Battle Over Self-Esteem

When I started thinking about this chapter, a very vivid picture came to mind: a pair of curmudgeonly old folks sitting on the sidelines of a kids' soccer game, moaning about how, in their day, kids didn't get these participation trophies to boost their self-esteem, and isn't that just the problem with kids these days, always needing their self-esteem boosted . . . ? At that point, it all turns into white noise for me.

I recognize that not all people of a certain generation feel this way, but it has been expressed by many. To understand the viewpoint, I turned to a family member who was firmly in the "no participation trophies" camp and asked him to tell me more about why this concerned him. His opinion was that if kids are given trophies for participating, they will, in his words, "need a reward for anything that they do, from flushing the toilet to cleaning up after themselves. Is that the kind of message we want to send them? That's not what the real world is going to be like."

Well he is right about that. (Especially for women, I'd add.) Still it's interesting how there can be so much fear of overinflating a child's self-esteem; yet once we become adults, this magical shift happens where we want and expect our self-esteem to be sky-high. In fact, I've heard the very same curmudgeonly folks who bemoan boosting kids' self-esteem switch to criticizing adults' choices because of their low self-esteem (e.g., "He drinks too much because he has no self-esteem.") That is confusing as hell, not to mention deeply sad to deprive children of positive reinforcement and acknowledgment of their strengths and accomplishments just when they are developing their sense of self.

During a recent family visit, a few family members commented on how beautiful our daughter was, with her sweet brown eyes and long, dark hair. (What can I say? She's adorbs.) These compliments were followed by, "We don't want to say too much because we don't want her to get a big head." Wait—why though? I think we all know how much we adults struggle to think highly of how we look—why would we not want to nurture this type of self-esteem in our children?

That said, I see a potential benefit in this viewpoint: by not smothering a kid in praise for their accomplishments or their other qualities, it leaves space for the kids themselves to notice and acknowledge that they just did a thing. Whether that thing was reading a list of books over the summer, finishing soccer camp, or earning the hallowed yellow belt in karate, just reaching a milestone in the learning process can be enough to strengthen their self-esteem. They can feel for themselves how their dedication paid off and recognize their capacity to work hard, finish what they start, and reach their goals. Ultimately, self-esteem is not contingent on accomplishments, but is built on a recognition of our unique strengths, personality traits, and self-image.

Believe me, I know the value of instilling a healthy sense of humility in children (and adults) and helping them recognize where they need to grow. We can do those things while also acknowledging their many beautiful facets, without qualification.

"She Must Have Low Self-Esteem"

Does that line sound familiar to you? I have often heard it when women's choices are being described, from the way they dress to the jobs they take to the people they date. I find it fascinating that a man's questionable choices are almost never chalked up to his lack of self-esteem. Equally fascinating is this belief that we can assess someone's self-esteem from the outside when it is such an internal experience. We don't go around saying that woman has "poor self-love" or "low self-care"; but for whatever reason, self-esteem is the concept that we have decided is acceptable to comment and place judgments on.

Let's go back and examine that reference from *Urban Dictionary*—the one that said self-esteem is "What every girl on *Girls Gone Wild* lacks." If you are unaware of the reference, *Girls Gone Wild* (*GGW*) was a reality video series in the nineties in which men videotaped young (hopefully of legal age, but who really knows?) women during spring break and other vacation-worthy occasions. The show's focus was capturing these women in moments of "wild" behavior like flashing the camera or dancing provocatively. I feel ambivalent about this reference precisely because I support women going out and doing whatever the hell they want—they deserve to have a great time without being sexualized by predatory shows like this. (I never thought I'd write a book with an extensive explanation of *GGW*, but here we are.)

Another thing I did not expect was getting into a long and heated debate with my husband about *GGW*. I shared the *Urban Dictionary* definition with him, followed by my long explanation of *GGW*, and waited for him to weigh in on the million-dollar question: *do* the women in *Girls Gone Wild* have low self-esteem? Instead, he latched onto my use of the word "predatory" when describing the show's premise. He argued that there was nothing predatory about this show—it just depicted women drinking and having a good time on vacation. I immediately launched into an angry tirade on informed consent and the inability to provide it when intoxicated, as the *GGW* women typically are. We went around and around, Michael telling me I needed to actually watch *GGW* (not just the commercials I saw as a child on channels I wasn't allowed to watch) to understand the context, me arguing that I didn't need to because I know not every woman on that show was in a state to consent to being recorded and likely did not even have their prefrontal cortex developed enough to know what they were consenting to.

What I finally realized amid our spirited debate is we have no real idea about the desires, intentions, or feelings experienced by the women depicted in *GGW*. Perhaps for some it was empowering and liberating to be a part of the show, while for others it may have been a deeply shameful experience they look back on with regret and despair. What is most important to me is society's reaction. The mainstream response to *GGW* reveals our tendency to assume that if a woman is behaving in a way that is unacceptable, immoral, or "unladylike," she must have low self-esteem. Think of comments in a similar vein that you might have heard:

- "She wears a lot of makeup because she has low self-esteem."
- "She dresses like that because she has poor self-esteem."
- "She sleeps with so many people because she has the worst self-esteem."

This isn't to say that men are never subject to this same external evaluation of their internal self-esteem. However, there is a complex layer of social pressures applied to how women act, dress, and behave, and when women disregard these pressures, we are painted with the "poor self-esteem" brush so heavily that we sometimes start to believe it ourselves. Rather than a deeply personal reflection of the parts of ourselves that matter the most to us, we rate our self-esteem based on other people's judgment of our appearance and behavior. Yuck.

Let's try a thought exercise that will help illuminate some of our explicit and implicit biases around women and their relationship with self-esteem. Read the sentence stems on the next page, take a moment to picture how each group of women act and how they look, then finish the sentences with whatever words come to mind.

Exercise

Women who have low self -esteem are ______________________

____

____

____

____

____

____

____

____

____

Women who have high self-esteem will ______________________

____

____

____

____

____

____

____

____

____

How do you feel about what you wrote down? Do you stand by it, or do you see some societal conditioning that makes you cringe?

Let me repeat this: you are not a reflection of your automatic thoughts. We each carry painful and at times ugly biases that don't align with our values. What's important is that we allow ourselves to see these blind spots so that we can understand how our self-esteem has been impacted. Remember that whatever assumptions you make about others' self-esteem, you're subconsciously applying those same standards to yourself.

With that in mind, what parts of this list do you want to keep, and what needs to be adjusted? Your self-esteem has far-reaching implications, from your perceptions of yourself and others to the actions you decide you are capable (or incapable) of taking to your mood and quality of life—let these implications be on *your* terms.

Self-Respect

Merriam-Webster Dictionary: *a proper respect for oneself as a human being; regard for one's own standing or position.*

Urban Dictionary: *It means being proud of who you are, even with the mistakes you made in the past. It means looking yourself in the mirror and thinking, "This guy has his shit straight." While you reflect on your past life, you should smile and think, "man I'm awesome." It means not using alcohol, drugs, or violence to solve problems. To overcome and oppress those who bring you down. Whatever hurts you only makes you stronger. It's to think that you are a good person, but not to the point of arrogance or narcissism. You don't have to be the smartest kid in your class, you don't have to make a million dollars a year, and you don't have to be popular to have self-esteem and self-respect.*

APA Dictionary of Psychology: *a feeling of self-worth and self-esteem, especially a proper regard for one's values, character, and dignity.*

8

SELF-RESPECT

Self-respect can easily get lost in the shuffle of the other self domains; it's particularly easy to confuse with self-esteem and self-worth. In fact, the top hits in my initial Google search of this term are various versions of the question, "How is self-respect different from self-esteem?" (Some links don't even bother to distinguish between the two.)

If self-respect is this neglected on Google, just imagine how easy it is to minimize or diminish in our own internal experience. Even the definition I find in the American Psychological Association's dictionary defines self-respect in terms of self-worth and self-esteem. (I find nothing more annoying than a definition that includes other broad concepts that need defining.) However, the social media platforms paint a much more helpful picture this time. Remember that we talked about how developing healthy selfishness meant prioritizing your needs consistently? Self-respect posts across Twitter, Instagram, and even TikTok are coming in hot on the pro-selfish (a.k.a. pro-you) stance:

- "The thing about self-respect is it's completely your own; no one can take it from you."
- "An apology without change is manipulation. Don't allow this for yourself."

- "I used to tolerate a lot because I didn't want to lose people . . . but IDGAF now. Boundaries."
- "Protect your peace. Be mindful who can access you."

Yes, yes, yes! IDGAFs aside, I am loving the way these posts encourage us to at least think about how our needs must factor into the actions and relational choices we make. Additionally, what feels different about the content of these posts versus the other self domains we've explored is these posts acknowledge that sometimes making the self-respectful choice can mean valuing your needs above others, whether it means restricting access to you or certain parts of you.

With social media being the double-edged sword it is, I also found some depictions of self-respect that weren't as favorable. "Have some self-respect" is a frequent refrain in post comments, particularly those aimed at women. I found this refrain in comments alluding to a woman's appearance ("How could you wear that? Have some self-respect!"), what a woman is eating ("How could you eat that? Have some self-respect!"), the music a woman is listening to, the opinions she expresses, even the decisions her children make.

It's incredibly disappointing when essential concepts related to our individual health are weaponized to shame us. Thus while we can applaud the self-respect posts that encourage self-focused behaviors and perspectives, it's worth being cautious about how we interpret these concepts based on their social media use.

Defining and Distinguishing Self-Respect

While self-esteem has to do with how we value and regard certain aspects of ourselves, self-respect has to do with a consistent acceptance of ourselves as we are now. For instance, I may not like that I have a strong desire to get to any place I'm going at least thirty minutes early. (What can I say? I just enjoy being settled into my space—making sure my water is filled up, maybe having a quick snack, scrolling through the social platforms until my appointment begins.) I may not value or even appreciate this part of me, but I do respect that it exists; because I do, I take time and effort to meet this need.

> Note that I did not take the time to convince myself this part of me is important and deserves to be liked, valued, or held in high esteem. I could do this, but, luckily, because I have decided I am deserving of respect, I don't need to like certain parts of myself or the needs they may have to act on them.

To clarify, self-respect does not mean responding to every need you have regardless of what it is. Instead self-respect means you can acknowledge and accept that these needs will require your attention and loving acceptance. For example, perhaps I have the desire to drink before I give a presentation in the hopes it will level off my anxiety. Healthy self-respect and the loving acceptance that comes along with it does not dictate that I find the nearest bar, but I acknowledge this desire instead while acting in a way that is congruent with my values.

For this reason, I consider self-respect to be most closely related to self-love. By respecting myself, I am pledging to treat myself with dignity and care. Similar to self-love, there are no conditions tied to this. No prerequisites that need to be met before this respect is given. However, this could lead us to our next debate as there is a philosophical divide on the question, "Should respect be given or earned?"

Should Respect Be Given or Earned?

Ah, the age-old question: Should respect be given or earned? In other words, are there conditions that need to be met before respect is given, or should respect just be a fundamental human right? My classic therapist response is, *it depends*. Specifically, it depends on your values.

On one hand, your belief system may teach that every human being is entitled to respect, regardless of their story, background, or relationship with you. On the other hand, experience may have taught you to view respect as a precious entity that is only given when it is earned. You may even land somewhere in between, as many people do. But when it comes to self-respect, the question to ask yourself is this: "Am I applying the same conditions for respecting others to myself?"

We can be downright contradictory in how we apply our rules to ourselves versus others. In asking this question about whether respect is given or earned, I'm not here to fundamentally change the way you understand respect, but to help you consider if you are giving yourself the same respect that you give others. I'm going to bet there's a gap there—let's see if we can fill it.

While we may differ in whether we believe respect should be given or earned, it is certainly true that we live in a society in which respect, particularly for women and minorities, must more often be earned than given. When we cannot rely on basic respect from the people, systems, and institutions around us, it becomes even more vital that we develop healthy self-respect for ourselves.

Teach Yourself Some Respect

Consider the lessons you have been taught about respect. I recall adages about respecting my elders through "being heard and not seen," or respecting my teachers by paying attention and being obedient. What I don't recall is being taught about how important it is to listen to and honor my own ideas, experiences, or feelings.

For all the good little girls who were taught to be respectful but not how to *be respected*, Aretha Franklin's mega-hit "Respect" is an introduction to a whole new way of being. Fun fact: The original version of the song was written and recorded by Otis Redding in 1965 as a man's declaration of his desires: "I'm about to give you all my money, and all I'm asking honey is to give me my propers." (What are "propers?" I'm not sure, but I think we can agree his wife does not owe him any for contributing to their shared household.) Franklin took this song, flipped the gender perspective, and created an electrifying ballad that became an anthem for the feminist and civil rights movements. Franklin was later quoted in her autobiography, *Aretha From The Roots* (1999), as saying that the song was "the need of a nation . . . the need of the average man and woman in the street, the businessman, the mother, the fireman, the teacher—everyone wanted respect."

Let us take a cue from the great Ms. Franklin: Even if we cannot always count on receiving respect from others, let us provide that respect to ourselves. It starts with taking the time we need to unpack any lessons that are getting in the way of developing a heathier relationship with the concept of self-respect.

The Golden Rule of Respect

I will always remember one consultation call that I had years ago, early in my career. A business owner contacted me about starting therapy to manage the guilt, anxiety, and fears she had about going back to work after having her first child. Man, I was excited! This is exactly the kind of client I love working with; consequently I went deep into her issues without paying attention to time or the proper boundaries of this initial consultation. Forty minutes later, it was the prospective client who finally broke in.

"So this is really helpful, and I want to keep going," she said, "but your time is important, and I want to respect it. Should we stop here for now?"

Thank goodness this happened over the phone—she did not see me turn three shades of red over being a therapist who forgot to respect her own boundaries. (We therapists are humans too!) Fortunately, this client and I did end up working together for years, but her response during our consultation has really stuck with me. As discussed, we cannot learn and develop healthy behaviors in isolation. When you are still working on developing respect for yourself, having someone show respect to you can be life-changing. (Thank you, clients—you will never know how much you teach your therapists!)

For that reason, I have a conflicted reaction to a "golden rule" formulation around respect. Knowing how powerful it can be to receive respect from others, I would never say that we should reserve our respect only for those who have clear respect for themselves. Still, it is true that the standard we set for ourselves will have an impact on how others treat us.

For example, while we all have a general standard for how we comport ourselves in someone else's home, some of our behavior is dependent on the standard they set. One friend of mine keeps her home spotless—not a dish in the sink, no clutter anywhere, not even a dog hair to be found on the furniture despite the presence of two very shaggy dogs. When I go to this friend's house, best believe I am respectful of the standard she sets. Following her lead, I remove my shoes, rinse my wineglass after drinking, and leave her home as perfect as it was when I entered.

Another friend of mine lives in a space I'd describe as a bit of a shit storm. Considering that she has three children and even more animals of various species (cats, dogs, I think even a ferret at some point), I understand that it's an uphill climb to keep things clean and organized. Anytime I stop by, I can expect to pick my way through clothes, toys, and pet supplies strewn across the floor, and be able to guess at least three of her meals that week by the amount of trash lying out. I recognize this sounds judgmental as hell, but the point is that her standard does affect the way I respect her space. I wish I could be that elevated person who is the same polite and considerate guest no matter where I am, but I'll admit that I follow her lead too, and thus find myself leaving my belongings around and not doing much to clean up after myself. While I am not intentionally disrespecting my friend's space, I'm instinctively calibrating my standard of respect toward her space based on how I perceive the standard she is setting.

If there is a golden rule of respect, I'd express it like this: we show others what respect looks like for us. Occasionally people may surpass that standard the way my client did; but if we are not clear on what our standard is, others will either follow our lead as they perceive it or, more dangerously, they'll decide how much and what kind of respect we deserve. For that reason, it is vital that we take the time to identify and communicate what self-respect means to us.

Building Self-Respect

By this point, I'm sure we can all agree that self-respect is important, especially for women. But there's a big difference between stating, for instance, "I respect my need as an introvert to take consistent time for myself," and actually supporting this need with daily, practical action. So let's explore how healthy, sustainable self-respect looks in action.

Self-Respect and Your Body

If there were any single area where nearly everyone could use more self-respect, it is toward their bodies. I'm sure you can easily list the ways you could improve your respect for your body—drink more water, get more sleep, eat nourishing food—yet how often and how consistently do you take those actions?

I suspect part of the challenge here is being fortunate enough to live as relatively healthy, able-bodied individuals. For many of us, there is a large period of life (from childhood to early adulthood) in which we can get away with prioritizing pleasure and busy-ness over the body's needs. Even as we get older and the demands on our time and energy increase, we often continue to expect optimal functioning without optimal input. While these expectations may be based on habits we have lived by for years, they can also represent a lack of self-respect for our evolving needs as we age.

Additionally, sometimes our feelings about our bodies impact the respect we show them. Like so many women, if I dislike the way my pants fit today, I may be less inclined to eat even when I feel hungry. Nevertheless, healthy self-respect compels me to honor the needs of my body regardless of how I look or feel. Unlike other *self* concepts, self-respect does not require liking ourselves; it simply means accepting and honoring ourselves because we deserve it.

> Eating is just one example; there are countless other ways in which we can show self-respect to our bodies. The simplest one is using the bathroom when we need to. I'm always shocked by the amount of time people will wait when nature calls. I remember more than one client mention to me that they actually peed themselves a little bit when they really needed to use the bathroom but did not feel like they could stop working.

I know it is not always easy to make the self-respectful choice toward your body, particularly when you are in settings that do not create conditions that make it easily accessible. However, these are the moments when self-respect shifts from a noun into a verb.

Self-Respect and Comparison

I've heard many clients self-critically state, "I know I shouldn't be comparing myself to another, but . . . " And cue the comparison.

My response is always, "Sure, it would be nice to not, but you are human. Of course you are going to compare yourself to others!"

Comparison is completely natural, even if it is fairly unpleasant. What's more, moments of comparison can become moments of insight if we allow ourselves to look through the lens of healthy self-respect.

I recall one client describing her envy of an older classmate who seemed perfectly comfortable and at ease in social situations. My client described being in awe of how this woman would seamlessly insert herself into conversations, seeming to always know the perfect thing to say that made everyone lean in closer. In comparison, my client felt that she was a "socially inept wall hugger" (her words) who, in the moments she did courageously join a group, brought the conversation to a crushingly awkward halt.

I explained to this client that self-respect did not necessitate that she should like or value the way she behaved in social settings compared to her classmate; rather, self-respect would move her to acknowledge and accept where she is now. To help her grasp the concept fully, I had her complete the following two sentence prompts:

If I respect how I am in this moment, that means I acknowledge:

(Example) Groups have never been easy for me. I don't particularly like being the center of a circle and prefer one-on-one contact with people instead.

If I show respect to myself and my internal experiences, that means I will: *(Example)* Allow myself to join the groups if I feel like it, but I can also seek out other people for more intimate conversations. Also, knowing that groups aren't easy for me, I can plan ahead to take short breaks, so I don't get overwhelmed.

Notice how self-respect helped the client focus on how she was feeling in the moment, versus negating her experiences or suspending relief until she developed certain social skills. Thanks to the inherent acceptance involved in self-respect, my client was eventually able to recognize that she did value her capacity to make deep one-on-one connections and, in fact, preferred to focus her efforts on those connections instead of developing a skill set for surface-level interactions.

That's the funny thing about comparison. There are certainly times when comparing ourselves to others can help us identify parts of ourselves we want to improve, but just as often, we find that the qualities we admire in others are not necessarily desirable to us. If we start from a place of self-respect, exploring comparisons can allow us to recognize and even admire the strengths we already have.

Self-Respect and Boundaries

Boundaries: another ubiquitous therapy term that people nod appreciatively at, but rarely take the time to examine in their actual lives. This is because boundary setting (and maintaining) is not easy—it requires careful consideration, hard conversations, adjusting to others' reactions, and more hard conversations to help process those reactions. But as challenging as they are, boundaries can be the clearest manifestation of self-respect.

I recall one client whose mother-in-law moved in with her and her partner two years into their marriage. This was a decision they had agreed on early in their relationship, and my client valued the cultural importance her partner placed on taking care of his mother as she aged. But as you might imagine, healthy boundaries in this relationship became very challenging and very necessary.

At first, my client relied on telling her partner when things about her mother-in-law bothered her: coming into their room without knocking, using personal items without asking, rarely pitching in to help with the housekeeping. While this strategy was somewhat effective, the principle of, "It's your family—you tell them," proved not to work so well with in-laws turned roommates.

In session after session, my client vented her frustrations, tallying up a long list of grievances toward her mother-in-law while feeling she could not advocate for herself because it would be perceived as prioritizing her needs over those of an elder. We discussed how self-respect and respect for others don't need to be mutually exclusive; how, without boundaries, respect toward others becomes hard to maintain; how examining what self-respect means to you can be the pathway for finding a respectful path forward.

Finally, we discussed what healthy self-respect meant to her—enjoying privacy, having a sense of safety with her belongings, working as a team in her household—and how it would look to acknowledge and honor her needs in her home without evaluating or assigning judgments to these needs. We utilized my earlier self-respect prompts:

If I respect how I am in this moment, that means I acknowledge: ___

(Example) I need to have privacy in my home. It's also important to me that everyone contributes in our household—no matter how big or small.

If I show respect to myself and my internal experiences, that means I will: *(Example)* Bring up the idea of a house meeting. We are all one family in one household now, which means new rules of engagement that need to be discussed.

Fortunately, the house meeting idea went over very well with my client's mother-in-law, probably because it was rooted in the same collectivist values that characterized her culture of origin. It took about seventeen house meetings before some of my client's boundaries finally stuck; but in the end, she saw progress!

Take a moment to consider for yourself a situation in your life that you would benefit from a dose from self-respect and fill out the following prompts.

Exercise

If I respect how I am in this moment, that means I acknowledge: __

If I show respect to myself and my internal experiences, that means I will: ____

Respected Women

As we've seen, developing healthy self-respect is not always an easy process. We live in systems, societies, and sometimes even families that make it challenging to cultivate and advocate for self-respect, particularly for women. The onus is on us as individuals to identify what self-respect means to us, to actualize this definition through consistent action, and to communicate our needs to others. We've learned enough about how to be respectable women; let's take the time to be respected women, especially by ourselves.

Self-Discipline

Merriam-Webster Dictionary: *Correction or regulation of oneself for the sake of improvement.*

Urban Dictionary: *The practice of dedicating oneself to the truth, delaying gratification, accepting responsibility, and having the capacity to plan for the future as well as being able to live in the moment.*

APA Dictionary of Psychology: *The control of one's impulses and desires, forgoing immediate satisfaction in favor of long-term goals.*

9

SELF-DISCIPLINE

When you consider the concept of self-discipline, what do you picture?

My mind goes to military recruits in boot camp, Olympic athletes, or medical school students—people who commit themselves to seemingly superhuman goals that require pushing their bodies, minds, and spirits to their very limits (or past these limits). Essentially, my idea of self-discipline is extreme, intense, possibly unrealistic and unsustainable. For that reason, when clients share their desire to work on developing self-discipline, I feel an immediate twinge of concern. While I wholeheartedly support their desire to build the habits needed to reach their goals, I worry about what extreme levels they hope to push themselves to.

But that's just my first thought. I want to pay more attention to my second thought, which says, *What if self-discipline doesn't have to be as polarizing and intense as I imagine it to be?* As we know by now, it's usually the things we have the greatest resistance to that reveal our deepest insights. If we take the time to truly understand what self-discipline means, we can learn how to develop a healthy relationship with it. Onward!

Defining Self-Discipline

If we examine the definitions at the beginning of this chapter, they all reflect a similar theme: that self-discipline entails forgoing immediate impulses and desires or applying certain corrections to our behaviors in favor of long-term gains. In short, self-discipline means making a hard choice for a good reason.

Consulting our social media sources, we find a similar theme:

- "You can either experience the pain of discipline or the pain of regret. The choice is yours."
- "Most of your problems are caused by a lack of self-discipline."
- "Self-discipline and self-reflection are other forms of self-love."
- "Self-discipline is the outward manifestation of your reality."

Same idea, with a little extra "tough love" emphasis—almost all the #selfdiscipline posts I found include the likelihood that you will experience something hard in pursuit of something ultimately beneficial. Another noteworthy finding from this search is that these posts look very different from the other topics we've explored thus far. When I searched #selfcare, #selfesteem, or #selflove, I was greeted by a variety of colors, fonts, and presentation styles, from trendy minimalism to the bright aesthetic of a preschool classroom. However, when I search #selfdiscipline, the posts almost all had the same color palette: black background, solid white font, occasionally a man's figure blurred out in the background. In case the visual design didn't make it clear that these posts were primarily targeted toward men, many of them included explicit hashtags like #menshealth or they referenced men in the caption.

I found this very interesting, especially considering how many posts on self-control were targeted toward women. Is it generally understood that women need to harness self-control while men need to harness self-discipline? When did self-improvement become so gendered?

In addition, both concepts seem to have a moral weight attached to them—a person lacking self-control is likely to be seen as amoral and maybe even dangerous, while a person lacking self-discipline is likely to be seen as lazy and even at fault for any of the problems they face.

Take a moment to consider what you have been taught about self-discipline that impacts your understanding of what healthy practice looks and feels like. When I think of my own history with self-discipline, I immediately think of my mother's trademark phrase: "Mind over matter." This phrase was used as an encouragement to finish our math homework when we were tired or to continue practicing tennis in the heat of Texas summers. "Mind over matter" was also invoked when I asked for some Hot Cheeto Fries before dinner, or for a restroom pit stop on a road trip. While the intention may have been different in each instance, the message I received was that being a good, disciplined girl meant to keep on keeping on even when I was tired, forgoing pleasure when I wanted it, and pushing forward even when I wanted a break. Not following "mind over matter" meant I was lazy, weak, and certainly not disciplined.

Again this may have not been the intention of my mother's phrase. However, considering our interpretations of the self-discipline messaging we've received can make us more attuned to the changes we hope to bring to our future.

Self-Discipline, Willpower, and Motivation

When clients share their desire to cultivate more self-discipline, one word comes up a lot: willpower.

"If I just had more willpower, I would be able to resist ordering Uber Eats as much."

"If I just had more willpower, I would make myself get up twenty minutes earlier to meditate."

"If I had more willpower, I could stay out of political arguments with my dad."

You get the gist. The thing is, willpower is finite. It may get you through one short-term challenge or help you push to the very end when your energy is completely zapped, but it is not a resource you can count on to sustain long-term change.

For example, it was sheer willpower that got me through the birth of my daughter. For some reason, I decided not to attend any birthing classes before the big day. Whatever was going to happen that day was going to happen, I thought, *Why try to prepare for an unpredictable experience?* As a result, after pushing for hours to the point of exhaustion, it was sheer willpower that enabled me to follow my nurse's direction to do "just one more push," over and over and over. (What a liar.)

Whether you've given birth, run a marathon, or just had to walk back to your car in insanely uncomfortable high heels, you know what I'm talking about. You're so far past your pain threshold that you can barely see straight, but somehow you summon the sheer willpower that propels you forward, knowing that once you reach the finish point, you are DONE. Without a doubt, willpower is great! However, just like positive affirmations, willpower is not something we can use to solve all our problems or to maintain long-term change.

That's where healthy self-discipline comes in. Unlike an eleventh-hour burst of willpower, self-discipline is based on making intentional, thoughtful, and at times difficult choices to take actions and follow paths that are congruent with our values, often at the expense of immediate gratification. It's that last part, the "expense of immediate gratification" part, that can really get in our way. One of the greatest challenges to self-discipline that comes up in my therapy sessions is the idea that we need motivation before we can begin to develop self-discipline.

At my first clinical practicum at a college counseling center, I recall multiple conversations with students who insisted that motivation was the secret ingredient they needed before they could do boring tasks like completing their homework or getting to class on time. I remember being so annoyed at these students—*obviously you aren't going to be motivated to do homework. It sucks, and you just do it anyway!* (I didn't last long in college counseling.)

In hindsight, I wish I had helped these clients explore this fallacy that many of us are brought up believing. Author Mark Manson sums it up well when he describes that, rather than motivation, it's *taking* action that spurs us to take action. That is to say, the first action we take inspires us to continue acting; as the results of our actions begin to pile up, we become more and more motivated. You might hate trig homework, but you make yourself do it for five minutes and realize, *Well, this isn't fun, but it's not terrible, and it's taking less time than I thought. I think I can get this done in the next hour for sure, and then I can go meet my friends on the quad.* There you go—self-discipline for the win!

I remember the "ah-ha!" moment I experienced the first time I grasped this. My clients felt demoralized, hopeless, and certainly unmotivated to do their homework, while I felt annoyed, bored, and unmotivated to help them. I didn't realize until that moment that we were all waiting for the same damn lightning bolt of inspiration.

This kind of thinking isn't just unproductive; it can be dangerous. When individuals are not able to summon enough willpower or motivation to take action and create change, it can lead them to think something is wrong with them, that they are inherently unable to reach their goals.

The Laziness Myth

Occasionally my college student clients laughed off my suggestions with the classic smart-kid excuse: "I'm just lazy." (I remember thinking, *Yep, sure sounds like it.*) Several years and thousands of client sessions later, I object anytime I hear this phrase from someone in therapy. I want to yell at them, "You are in therapy! Does this feel like something a lazy person does?"

Hopefully you already know that you are not lazy—if you were, why would you be reading this book? (A lazy person would read something much more entertaining, with far fewer exercises.) But in case you do hold this belief about yourself in other areas of your life, you may have had thoughts like these:

- *Why can't I get up in the morning to work out? Because I'm lazy.*
- *Why can't I get up in the morning to write? Because I'm lazy.*
- *Why can't I cook more at home instead of ordering takeout every night? Because I'm lazy.*
- *Why can't I get more done at work? Because I'm lazy.*

My response to these comments is simple: humans are wired to preserve our energy. Back in our caveman days, we didn't know when our next meal would be available and were frequently confronted by threats to our safety. Consequently, in between scavenging for food or fighting for our lives, we needed to maintain our precious energy so that we could forage and fight another day. For better or worse, that aspect of our brain function is still present. Our automatic choice will almost always be the path that takes the least energy—sleeping more, doing less. It's an evolutionary reality, not a moral failing.

Now here's where I'm going to blow your mind. If we can accept that we will usually lean toward the path that requires the least energy, we can create goals and action plans that work *with* this reality versus against it.

This is the definition of healthy self-discipline: working with our existing emotions, impulses, and energy level to make choices that move us in our desired direction.

The Energy Drain of the Women's Tax

As women, our biological wiring to preserve energy is complicated by a particularly draining experience known as the women's performance tax (or just the "women's tax"). This term, coined by the countless research studies that have confirmed this phenomenon, refers to the extra effort required of women to prove they are equal in value to their male colleagues (King, 2020). This is especially true for women of color.

Thanks to being perceived as less competent compared to their male (especially white, heterosexual male) counterparts, women bear the brunt of their workplace's energy-draining tasks. We don't do it because we like it, but because there is a constant fear of falling behind our peers on a scale that is inherently imbalanced.

The performance tax doesn't end at the workplace—it follows women into other domains of life as well. For example, when I first became a parent, I was stressed about caring for my daughter as she deserved, but I was equally worried about rising to the higher standard of parenting I knew I'd be held to. While it was acceptable and even humorous for my husband to make mistakes or not know what to do, I often felt like my confusion was not received with the same understanding or grace.

While it's encouraging to see workplace (and parenting) inequity being confronted with the reality of women's lived experiences, it's vital that we acknowledge this systemic challenge to developing healthy self-discipline. We'll never create or maintain healthy self-discipline if we measure ourselves by the constantly shifting standard that society holds for women.

How Our Brains Make Self-Discipline Hard

Just as we need to be aware of the biological and social challenges to the development of healthy self-discipline, we also need to explore the very real (and very human) pleasure-seeking parts of ourselves that can get in our way. Just as our brains are wired to seek the least energy-draining path, they are also wired to flood us with dopamine when we are presented with a pleasurable option. For example, I have a very visceral reaction when I even think of ordering Frenchy's fried chicken for dinner instead of cooking from scratch (or using up leftovers). I'm not exaggerating when I say my mind and body feel pulled like a magnet toward Frenchy's.

This is where healthy self-discipline enters the picture. I don't berate myself for the wish to gobble some Frenchy's, or for the desire to follow the path of least energy drain. Instead, I give myself full permission to feel less than overjoyed about the choice to forgo immediate gratification *while still making the choice,* because it's more in line with my values for being healthy, being financially responsible, and being an active parent (because eating Frenchy's puts me in a food coma).

The real energy drain in this situation isn't cooking a healthy meal—it's fighting with my impulses and desires. Here's a dramatized version of how that argument would have gone:

> *Damn, I'm hungry . . . and Frenchy's sounds really good. But ugh, we have all those leftovers, and I did plan to make quesadillas with them. Why do I always want to eat out? What is wrong with me? I make this big deal with Michael about saving money and then I'm the one always saying we should eat out. Sigh—I just don't feel like cooking, especially after the day I've had. Of course, I doubt eating Frenchy's and then vegging on the couch is going to make me feel better. I am so damn lazy. Whatever—I'll just do the quesadillas. This sucks. I suck.*

Do you see how, no matter which choice I make, I've burned a lot of precious energy berating myself for my desires? It's the same type of inner monologue my clients share with me. Worse, when we put ourselves in opposition to our impulses and desires, we end up making choices based on a makeshift point system, rather than based on our values. In this situation, I overcame my desires and decided to go with the healthy choice, but the way I went about it makes it a lot easier to cave next time I am faced with this decision, *Well, I did such a good job beating my desires last time, so this time I deserve to eat out.* This kind of thinking pits you against yourself, challenging you to see how "superhuman" you can be in resisting your own desires one time, then setting you up to "fail" the next time. This can easily begin the kind of deprivation-binge cycles that lead to or reinforce disordered eating.

Additionally, this same cycle can occur with other kinds of behaviors you are hoping to reinforce. For example, because I resisted my desire to stay up late Wednesday night and went to sleep early, I'm going to give myself more runway to stay up late Thursday evening. Similarly, I really focused last week and worked on that presentation for a solid two hours. Now I can take a break for the next two weeks. Creating this internal point system between your willpower and your goals can lead you down a slippery slope in which your actions are dependent on the results of the previous day rather than your intentions and wishes today.

Thus, whether you go to bed on time, work on your presentation, or eat the Frenchy's is way less important to your self-discipline than how you got there. Instead of framing your goals and intentions in opposition to your impulses and desires, let's explore how they could all work together. After all, your impulses and desires aren't going anywhere.

Realistic Habit-Building for Healthy Self-Discipline

Start your search into self-discipline, and you'll be rewarded with a wealth of tips and tricks for how to build habits. Habits are the building blocks of healthy self-discipline for the simple reason that they conserve our energy. The more we become habituated to a certain task, the less willpower it requires from us, to the point that we can eventually complete that task while planning our weekend and playing with the dog at the same time.

Habits are great! They are also hard as hell to implement and even harder to really make stick. Fortunately, tons of research is out there on the best, most efficient, and longest-lasting ways to build habits. My all-time favorite habit-building book is *Atomic Habits* by James Clear (2018). The wonderful thing about this book is that Clear's techniques encourage us to work with our impulses, wishes, and desires instead of against them. While I could do a whole book report on his amazing book, I will instead recommend you read it yourself, and I will just share the top two pieces of guidance that I find most helpful.

1. Make it easy

Knowing our biological instinct to preserve energy, Clear recommends that when you are trying to create a habit, make the action easy. The reverse also applies: when you are trying to break a habit, make the action hard. For example, if I am trying to create a habit of going for a walk each day, I will put my tennis shoes in my office so that I can immediately lace up and walk out the door, rather than spend time searching for my shoes. Yes, it's ridiculously easy to go find my shoes, but it's even easier to not go on a walk when my shoes are in another room. On the flip side, if I am trying to stop checking my phone during team meetings, I might throw my phone across the room (and hope it lands on a pillow). While I still can get up and reclaim my phone, I've just added a step that makes this a little bit harder. Such simple shifts, but they can be so powerful!

2. Stack your habits

I love Clear's concept of habit stacking—it means taking your desired habit and implementing it between two already well-established habits. For instance, I've had the goal to learn Spanish for years, and even downloaded one of those apps that make learning a language seem super doable. The only problem was that I could never get myself to consistently use the app. I thought about it a lot, and wasted a fair amount of energy getting mad at myself for not doing it, even creating fantasy commitments like, "I'll start using the app when my daughter is sleeping through the night consistently . . . ," which later became, "I'll start when she consistently sleeps until 7:00 a.m."

Enter habit stacking. First I identified what part of the day I might ideally want to work on learning Spanish—I decided on mornings, because what could be more delightful than some language learning over coffee? Next I chose two well-established morning habits to "stack" between this new one—making coffee and scrolling through my social platforms of choice. I'd get up, make my coffee as I always do, open the language app and go through a lesson, then move on to Instagram. Today, the sound of the coffee drip has become an automatic cue for my daily Spanish lesson.

Now it's your turn! Take a moment to consider one habit you would like to introduce into your life. Make it as concrete and tangible as you can (e.g., instead of "meditating more," think "use my meditation app for five minutes each morning"). Now consider the time of day you would like this habit to happen and the two existing habits you could sandwich it between.

Exercise

Existing habit: ______________________________

____

____

____

____

____

Habit I want to create: ______________________________

____

____

____

____

____

Existing habit: ____

____

____

____

____

____

One thing I could do to make this habit easier to create: __________

____

____

____

____

____

Be prepared for there to be challenges and slips along the way. If you encounter a slip, go back to the "Make it easy" step. Identify what challenges are getting in your way and problem solve how you can make this habit even simpler and less energy draining for yourself. As a bonus, use another edict from Clear's book to "Make it attractive." If you are finding it hard to take that walk outside, even with your shoes right next to your desk, download your favorite podcast episode ahead of time to make the idea of a walk even more tantalizing. Again let's work with the way your mind, impulses, and desires work.

The development of these skills to cultivate healthy self-discipline is important, because many of the things we desire that are vital to our mental health, such as being active, sleeping well, or working toward personal and professional goals include hardship, challenges, and the precious resource of our energy. Self-discipline allows us to meet these challenges with intentionality, grace, and efficiency.

Self-Leadership

Merriam-Webster Dictionary: *No definition available*

See "self-directed," meaning directing oneself or capable of directing oneself.

Urban Dictionary: *No definition available.*

APA Dictionary of Psychology: *The extent to which individuals are goal-oriented and resourceful.*

10

SELF-LEADERSHIP

You may be thinking, "We are ending on a chapter that doesn't even have a definition?" Hey, I did my best. *Urban Dictionary* certainly isn't any help and even *Merriam-Webster* doesn't have an official definition of self-leadership. Fortunately, we can turn to the field of psychology—specifically, internal family systems (IFS), the model we introduced way back in Chapter 1. To refresh your memory, this model of psychotherapy describes individuals as a system of parts, each with valuable core properties, which were all created to serve a purpose.

IFS also posits that we have a Self, which is not a part, but rather, our very being and consciousness. The goal of IFS is to empower individuals to be Self-led, meaning that each of us is the caretaker, shepherd, and ultimately the leader of all the different parts of ourselves. The Self is capable of integrating all our different parts to allow us to be whole.

IFS describes that when we are in Self energy, we experience any of the following: creativity, calm, compassion, connectedness, confidence, courage, clarity, and (my personal favorite) curiosity. If you want to step into Self energy so that you can move into self-leadership, the easiest way to do so is by exercising some curiosity. Simply ask yourself, "What do I notice right now?" or "What part of me seems most dominant?" or "How do I feel toward this part?" and you'll step into the role of Self. Once you are in that position, you can determine how to lead your system of parts.

Along the journey of this book, you may have encountered parts of yourself that you enjoyed, such as the parts that care for you and others, or the parts that have meaningful dreams and goals. You may have also encountered parts of yourself that are annoying as hell and get in the way of being the kind of person you strive to be. (I'm looking at you, people-pleasing part.) Self-leadership requires the recognition that all these parts can serve us, but they need our care, guidance, and support to do so. One last time, let's all pause and remember Esmerelda.

Think of self-leadership as being the parent to little children. While some parts may really get under your skin, they are still part of your family and need your loving guidance to become a supportive part of the system. That's the goal with self-leadership: by providing our parts with the care and direction they need, we unburden them from their maladaptive roles and allow them to participate in the "family" in a way that aligns with our values and wishes.

If you are wondering what specific steps you can take to foster self-leadership, look no further than all the exercises and reflections in this book! If you have tried them, you've already worked through several of the components that add up to self-leadership:

- You've learned to exercise the unconditional **self-love** that allows you to take the challenging steps and feel loved even when you make the inevitable fuckup.
- You've learned to practice **self-care** so that you feel nourished enough to reach your goals, but more importantly because you deserve to be taken care of.
- You've learned to cultivate **self-trust** so that you believe in your own ability to create the life you desire, even and especially when it feels impossible.
- You've learned how **self-control** can help you manage the very understandable impulses, desires, and wishes that make life challenging.

- You've learned **self-talk** techniques that inspire and fuel you, while also recognizing that even when you can't control that internal monologue, you can control what you pay attention to.
- You've learned that you need to be **selfish** sometimes, because you are the only one who truly understands what you need, and there is a whole family of parts that rely on you.
- You've learned to nurture your **self-esteem,** because your less-desirable parts only become dominant and get out of hand when something important (a part of yourself that you value most) is threatened.
- Finally you've learned the importance of developing healthy **self-discipline** that allows you to make the tough choices that align with your values and get you where you want to go.

You may be thinking, *I already have an actual family that I have to lead. Now I am being asked to be the leader of all my parts?* Short answer: Yes. Remember, one of the key reasons we need to be selfish is because no one else knows us or our needs as well as we do. Similarly, we are the only ones who can be the leaders of our parts. Our partners, colleagues, caregivers, and others in our close circle can certainly contribute to the healing, nurture, and care of our parts. Still, at the end of the day, we are ultimately in charge of ourselves. And isn't that how we want it anyway?

Leading Your Own Way

As women, we are often tasked with so many default roles in the different systems we inhabit. We are not just professionals, partners, and parents—we are also tasked with unofficial roles like life coach, crisis support system, social coordinator, parenting consultant, and so many other unacknowledged (and certainly unpaid) roles. Knowing how to infuse self-leadership into all these different parts of our lives can feel impossible. So let's break it down.

The Selfish Professional

Now is an interesting time to consider what it means to be a selfish professional. We are in the aftermath of the "Great Resignation"—that is, the mass exodus of people from their workplaces in the aftermath of the pandemic's first big wave. Presumably, the mass trauma of 2020 reminded people that their needs, and the needs of their family, outweighed the demands of their jobs. There is endless variety in what led folks to leave their workplaces, but in general, I consider these folks brave as hell for making this leap. For me, they serve as a model of what it means to be a selfish professional.

The selfish professional prioritizes her needs, desires, and career aspirations when she makes career decisions. She recognizes that just as she benefits from her job, her job also benefits from her being there . . . and not just within the role for which she was hired. Research suggests that, regardless of the size of the company, women are tasked with playing many unofficial and unrecognized roles (King, et al., 2020). These may include tasks like mentoring younger employees, supporting their younger coworkers, or social planning for birthdays, baby showers, work anniversaries, and office parties. These responsibilities might seem frivolous (which is likely why they get shuffled off on women in the first place); but in reality, they go a long in way in creating a workplace where individuals feel recognized and, as a result, remain loyal and productive. The Party Committee doesn't sound so frivolous when you look at it that way, does it?

In smaller companies, women may even take on positions that ought to be actual jobs. For example, I know many women who essentially crafted their workplace's parental leave policy from scratch, because they were the first ones in the company to experience pregnancy and require parental leave. They had to spend valuable time researching, drafting, and educating others on this plan while still maintaining the responsibilities of their job . . . and let's not forget navigating the daily challenges of pregnancy!

Being a selfish professional means informing others that these roles are vital to the workplace and deserve to be acknowledged and compensated (through title or pay, but hopefully both). Alternatively, if you decide these roles are not aligned with your values or interests, being a selfish professional means deciding not to partake in these roles.

Of course, women who willingly accept these roles may encounter resistance from their companies against acknowledging their extra contribution. One woman I worked with described how her workplace seemed completely unwilling to recognize the diversity and inclusion gaps in their environment. After speaking to leadership about her concerns but receiving no support, she decided to start a workplace book club specifically to help foster learning about others' experiences.

The book club ended up being wildly successful, growing in number and even splitting off into subgroups on specific topics. It also took a shitload of time to manage. Once again, my client sought out leadership's support, asking them to recognize the impact of what she created and the need for additional ways to foster a safe and inclusive work environment. While she was praised for her initiative and for the positive impact of the book club, leadership still refused to make any changes to company policies; they also refused to take anything off my client's plate to allow her to continue in this unofficial but demonstrably important role.

This was a painful values conflict for my client. She debated between her desire to support her fellow coworkers' learning and growth and her need to protect her own time, worth, and value. The word "selfish" came up several times in her internal debate—she felt that she was abandoning her coworkers, several of whom she counted as close friends. Ultimately she decided to leave her workplace for an organization that hired her not only for her professional skill set, but specifically for her talent in creating workplace cultures where others felt supported, safe, and empowered. Her selfish choice was rewarded with a position in which she is fully resourced to make an impact on others at a higher scale than she ever had in her previous job.

I hope what you take from this story is that what you bring to your workplace matters. If your gifts are not fully recognized at work, you deserve more. If helping others is the motivation you need to make a difference, consider how your ability to make an impact could skyrocket if you worked at a company that fully recognizes and supports your gifts.

Take a moment to consider your own position at work. What tasks, responsibilities, and roles take the majority of your time? What tasks, responsibilities, and roles would you *love* to take most of your time? If you find lots of overlap between those answers, you're in the right place! If not, this is the time to consider some selfish choices that could create a difference in your career. While there will always be parts of our job that we don't enjoy (I will always hate charting), we deserve to work where we feel supported and valued—somewhere we enjoy at least *most* of the time.

Speaking of being supported, a vital aspect of this conversation is financial support and security. I recognize that making drastic decisions, like leaving your job, is not always realistic when you have bills to pay and mouths to feed. Nevertheless, I want to challenge you to think about a selfish choice you *could* make in your current professional reality. For example, perhaps you can't quit your job entirely, even though it is not valuing you in the way you deserve, but you can commit to devoting one hour a week to career planning (i.e., resumé updating, job searching, networking with others) to start planning your next move.

Here are some examples of other choices a selfish professional may make:

- I will stop responding to my email the minute my day is over. If there is an emergency, someone can call me. (Hot tip: put that in your signature line so folks know you will not be responding until you return to the office.)

- I will do what is asked of me on a given project; not one extra measure of effort will be given. (Oh man, this can be hard for us overachievers . . . but you can do it!)
- I will not volunteer for any additional projects outside of my scope of work. I will sit in that awkward silence for however long I need to until someone else volunteers.
- I will ask for help, not only when I feel completely overwhelmed and burned out, but even when I feel that extra support would be beneficial to me.
- I will offer others *only* the time spots I have available and resist the urge to flex my boundaries, even when I know my needs may cause annoyance and inconvenience to others.

Exercise

Insert your selfish professional move here: ____________________

The Selfish Parent

Ah, the selfish parent. Sounds like an oxymoron, right? Instead of describing what I think a selfish parent entails, let me show you.

When Michael and I returned to work after parental leave, we started our daughter in childcare on Mondays, Wednesdays, and Fridays. On Tuesdays and Thursdays, Michael and I switched off taking care of our daughter during the workday. I really loved the idea that our daughter would be at home with at least one of her parents two days out of the work week—*how awesome*, I thought, *that she was at home with her parents more days than not. What a beautiful, modern working family we were!*

Unfortunately, this schedule was terrible for both Michael and me. On Tuesdays, I started my day with sessions as early as 6:30 a.m. while Michael was with our daughter, then we frantically switched her off, so Michael could start his day at 9:30 a.m. At that point, I was with her until my evening sessions started at 4:00 p.m. For me, it felt like a twelve-hour workday.

We decided to enlist childcare on Tuesdays and Thursdays. This made my work schedule much easier, but it also meant I had to give up my fantasy of having our daughter with us more days than not during the week. Michael and I *could* have kept functioning that way—it was stressful, but not overwhelmingly so—but we simply didn't want to. It felt like a selfish move, because it was one.

We don't have to wait till we are past our breaking point to ask for things to be different. (At that point, it's not a selfish choice—it's a necessary choice for survival.) Yes, it was selfish to prioritize our desire to have a less stressful workday over time we could spend with our daughter. It was also the right move for our family. In short, don't wait for shit to really hit the fan before making the changes you need.

Of course, women have a unique challenge to being a selfish parent—namely, the idea that mothers should want to be mothering at all times. Michael and I used to get into a recurring argument over how to split up morning baby duties. As a natural early riser, I fell into the role of being primary morning parent. But while I am okay doing this most of the time (with some healthy martyr attitude of course), I certainly would like some mornings that are all my own. The first morning we made the switch, Michael was surprised and a little peeved that I still got up as early as I always did and spent the morning enjoying a leisurely cup of coffee and reading a magazine while he looked after our baby. While he did want to support me having some mornings to myself, he didn't understand why I couldn't be the one to take care of our daughter if I was already going to be awake. Didn't I enjoy spending time with her? Is she a chore?

My answer was, "Yes, I love spending time with her and yes, taking care of her, especially in a way that aligns with our values, is a chore." (I found myself rewriting that last sentence over and over as I struggled to reconcile my near-bursting level of love for my daughter with my near-bursting need for alone time.) Even though I *could* wake up with my daughter each morning and feel deeply grateful that I have the opportunity to do so, I still selfishly choose my own time every once in a while. Believe me, everyone benefits from this choice. What's more, I hope that as my daughter gets older, she notices that it's sometimes her dad who gets her up and takes care of her in the morning, not because her mom is rushing to work or has to go meet someone else, but because her mom values herself enough to focus on herself sometimes.

What selfish choice would you like to make as a parent? To help you brainstorm, consider what you'd like to do more of, if you had one more hour in the day. Then find a way to enlist your partner or your support squad (paid or not) to help you make this happen. Your mind will likely throw up some immediate resistance to this idea, naming all the reasons that this won't work, will be too hard, or will inconvenience others. Name all the "yes, buts" without fighting against them, then let yourself start generating some creative solutions that can make your selfish choice a reality.

The Selfish Partner

This section is for you, whether you are in a relationship or not. Use it to reflect on your past relationships and consider how you want to show up in future partnerships.

I'm pretty sure that if I told the couples I work with that they needed to be more selfish partners, the response would be split. One partner would say, "Hell yes, this is what I've been talking about!" while the other would say, "Fuck this. We're finding a new therapist."

Being a selfish partner often feels inherently contradictory to fostering healthy, loving relationships. Yet by being lovingly selfish partners, we can create relationships that are nurturing and responsive to the individual needs of each partner and thus, the needs of the couple.

Let's unpack this further. In Psychobiological Approach to Couples Therapy (PACT), clinician Stan Tatkin discusses the concept of "managing thirds" in a relationship. A "third" is anything or anyone outside of the relationship—it could include children, in-laws, or pets, as well as careers, hobbies, even addictions, just to name a few. Thirds may often intrude on the needs and health of the couple; therefore, it is up to the couple to manage their thirds in a way that supports the needs of both partners and thus fosters a healthy relationship. An important note here is that thirds will always be the responsibility of *both* partners to manage, versus the sole responsibility of just one partner. As annoying as your partner's feisty Chihuahua is, he is also your third to deal with.

Here's another example from my own life: Michael has cycled through a ton of hobbies in our relationship, but there are a couple that have really stuck around for years and have provided him with heaps of joy, as well as taking up heaps of his time. Early in our relationship, I found the amount of time he spent on his hobbies annoying and even intrusive on our relationship. Ultimately though, I decided his hobbies were his problem, and I could find equally fulfilling things to do on my own (read: new TV shows). However, as these hobbies continued to take a prominent role in our relationship, with woodworking classes taking up weekends or evenings spent pursuing trading cards on eBay,

I realized my standoffish approach to Michael's hobbies wasn't really working for me. And if it wasn't working for me, it meant his hobbies were not working for our relationship. (Tip: anytime something is not working for one partner, this means it is not working for either of you. Period.) Managing this third in a healthy way meant discussing what these hobbies meant to Michael and finding ways to incorporate them in his life while also ensuring they did not infringe on our time together as a couple.

Being a selfish partner means doing what you want to do regardless of what your partner wants or how they feel. Being a lovingly selfish partner means taking the time to identify what you care about most for yourself—your hobbies, your values, your passions, or just your favorite things that keep you fulfilled and content—then enlisting your partner's support to make it happen.

As always, there's a special note here for women. We've already discussed how women often struggle to advocate for our needs, especially if we worry that it may infringe on the needs or desires of others. Another issue is how we understand selfishness. Time and time again, I hear women describe how selfish they are because they have to work late or need more support from their partner because of work demands. Time and time again, I say, "Can we stop calling it selfish when it's for work?" This is not the kind of selfish behavior I'm advocating for. Instead, I encourage you to be selfish when it comes to the things you love, are curious about, are interested in. They don't have to be profound or productive or anything at all.

Take Cameron, who had a deep love of birding. What a wonderfully specific and quite adventurous hobby, not to mention a great example of a third to manage! The thing about birding is that can't be done in the privacy of your home once the day is over. It requires time, planning, and trips to different places around the world based on bird migration patterns. Cameron could have just told her partner, Troung, that she was going on her birding trip to Colombia even though it interfered with his parents' anniversary celebration. But again, being a selfish partner does not mean a blatant disregard for everyone and everything. The lovingly selfish move would be for Cameron to share how important this trip is to her and to let Troung know that she needs his help in making it happen. For Cameron, this ask brought up intense discomfort as she recognized how upset and uncomfortable it could make Troung, yet she asserted her needs anyway because: 1) she is an empowered self-leader, and 2) she knows the alternative is a slow build of resentment that would eventually swallow her relationship whole.

What thirds have you brought into your relationship? Perhaps it's your pet, your children, your hobby, or your faith. After reading the examples, use the following prompts to consider your thirds, understand their importance to you, and enlist your partner in managing them with you.

A third I have brought into my relationship that I truly care about is . . . *(Example)* playing with remote control cars.

If I could be a little more selfish in my relationship as I nurture this third, you would see me . . . *(Example)* take steps to fulfill my dream of building my own RC car, even though it is time-consuming and takes up a good amount of physical space.

To make this happen, I'm going to enlist my partner's help in . . . *(Example)* clearing out a space in the garage that I'll call "Jess's RC Shop." I also want to find a way to build some RC time into our schedules, versus waiting till everyone is asleep and I'm too tired to enjoy myself.

Exercise

A third I have brought into my relationship that I truly care about is . . . ______

If I could be a little more selfish in my relationship as I nurture this third, you would see me . . . ______

To make this happen, I'm going to enlist my partner's help in . . . ______

One Last Challenge

In closing, I'd like to quote another notable post I saw in my social media research that expresses my final hopes for you:

"I wish women were as selfish as y'all give us credit for."

Over the year of writing this book, I had many conversations with women about the content I planned to include. I got a lot of head nods as I described the need to disentangle core psychological concepts from the distorted versions on social media. I received some reassuring chuckles as I described my long-winded analogies of Esmerelda, my protective manager part, and my description of the epic battle between positive and negative thinking. But one of my favorite reactions is the one I got when I simply share the title of the book. Women were instantly intrigued, some laughed, many raised their eyebrows, and almost all said, "Now that's a book I want to read." I found it fascinating that across age groups, stages of life, and career paths, women were primed and ready to learn how to be more selfish. It's always good to learn that the theme of your book lands with people after you've written nine chapters about it.

Now that I know the interest is there, I'm fantasizing about a world in which all the women around me lean into their self-relationship, take the time to understand all the parts of themselves that may go unseen, and develop a mode of self-leadership that allows them to live as the women they have always dreamed of being. Doesn't it sound glorious?

I know this fantasy is not without flaws. One of the reasons this book starts with self-love is because we humans have a built-in "stumble" feature. We are going to fuck up time and time again, but the hope is that we have enough self-love and self-trust to allow ourselves to keep trying to figure it out and do the next right thing. (Yes, I lifted that line from *Frozen 2*. If you're a parent, you get it.) And that is part of my fantasy too: that women know they matter enough to give themselves a second, third, or seventh chance to pursue the things they care about, even when their choices don't gel easily with the wishes or needs of those around them. A crucial aspect of this fantasy is that we recognize that we are worthy of disrupting the peace, the system, and maybe even ourselves a little bit.

I imagine you didn't pick up this book while looking for a way to be a little more comfortable in your life as it is; hopefully you were intrigued by the possibility of more: more focus on yourself, more space for yourself, more of the time and attention from yourself that you deserve. Being selfish is a challenge—like anything worth having, it takes work! This work does not end once you reach the end of this book; it must be woven into your mindset, incorporated into your decision-making, and revisited as you and your life continue to evolve. It's hard, but it's worth it. Do this work for your values, for your family, for your passions, and for the other women in your life who look up to you.

Most importantly, do it for yourself.

REFERENCES

Borenstein, J. (2020, July 9). *Self-Love and what it means.* Brain & Behavior Research Foundation. https://www.bbrfoundation.org/blog/self-love-and-what-it-means

Bowlby, J. (1979). The Bowlby-Ainsworth attachment theory. *Behavioral and Brain Sciences, 2*(4), 637–638. https://doi.org/10.1017/S0140525X00064955

Brown, B. (2018). *Dare to lead: Brave work. Tough conversations. Whole hearts.* Random House.

Brown, J. D., & Marshall, M. A. (2006). The three faces of self-esteem. In M. Kernis (Ed.), *Self-esteem: Issues and answers* (pp. 4–9). New York: Psychology Press.

Cerrato, J., & Cifre, E. (2018). Gender inequality in household chores and work-family conflict. *Frontiers in Psychology, 9,* 1330. https://doi.org/10.3389/fpsyg.2018.01330

Chapple, C. L., Pierce, H., & Jones, M. S. (2021). Gender, adverse childhood experiences, and the development of self-control. *Journal of Criminal Justice,* 74, Article 101811.

Clear, J. (2018). *Atomic habits: An easy & proven way to build good habits & break bad ones.* Penguin.

DeMarree, K. G., & Rios, K. (2014). Understanding the relationship between self-esteem and self-clarity: The role of desired self-esteem. *Journal of Experimental Social Psychology, 50,* 202–209. https://psycnet.apa.org/doi/10.1016/j.jesp.2013.10.003

Giuntella, O., Hyde, K., Saccardo, S., & Sadoff, S. (2021). Lifestyle and mental health disruptions during COVID-19. *Proceedings of the National Academy of Sciences, 118*(9), Article e2016632118. https://doi.org/10.1073/pnas.2016632118

Hempel, R. J., Booth, R., Giblin, A., Hamilton, L., Hoch, A., Portner, J., . . . & Wolf-Arehult, M. (2018). The implementation of RO DBT in clinical practice. *The Behavior Therapist, 41*(3), 161–173.

King, M. P. (2020). *The Fix: Overcome the invisible barriers that are holding women back at work.* Atria Books.

King, T., Hewitt, B., Crammond, B., Sutherland, G., Maheen, H., & Kavanagh, A. (2020). Reordering gender systems: Can COVID-19 lead to improved gender equality and health? *The Lancet, 396*(10244), 80–81. https://doi.org/10.1016%2FS0140-6736(20)31418-5

LeanIn.Org. (2021). *Women in the workplace.* https://leanin.org/women-in-the-workplace/2021/the-state-of-women-in-america

Linehan, M. M. (1993). Dialectical behavior therapy for treatment of borderline personality disorder: Implications for the treatment of substance abuse. *NIDA Research Monograph, 137*, 201–201.

Lynch, T. R. (2018). *The skills training manual for radically open dialectical behavior therapy: A clinician's guide for treating disorders of overcontrol.* New Harbinger Publications.

Parasurama, P., Sedoc, J., & Ghose, A. (2022). Gendered information in resumes and hiring bias: A predictive modeling approach. *SSRN.* https://dx.doi.org/10.2139/ssrn.4074976

Schwartz, R. C., & Sweezy, M. (2019). *Internal family systems therapy.* Guilford Publications.

Tronick, E. D., Als, H., & Brazelton, T. B. (1977). Mutuality in mother-infant interaction. *Journal of Communication, 27*(2), 74–79. https://doi.org/10.1111/j.1460-2466.1977.tb01829.x

Tulshyan, R., & Burey, J. A. (2021, February 11). *Stop telling women they have imposter syndrome.* Harvard Business Review. https://hbr.org/2021/02/stop-telling-women-they-have-imposter-syndrome

ABOUT THE AUTHOR

Sunita Osborn, PsyD, MA, is a writer and licensed psychologist who practices in Houston, Texas, and works with adults and couples. Dr. Osborn is a trauma-informed and attachment therapist with specialized training in couples therapy and reproductive mental health. She has a specialty and passion for working with women facing anxiety, depression, fertility issues, relationship struggles, and all the many challenges and unique experiences that come along with being a woman in the current day.